GREATEST MOMENTS IN
BASEBALL

GREATEST MOMENTS IN
BASEBALL

JOEL ZOSS

Exeter Books

NEW YORK

A Bison Book

First published in USA 1987 by Exeter Books
Distributed by Bookthrift
Exeter is a trademark of Bookthrift Marketing, Inc.
Bookthrift is a registered trademark of Bookthrift Marketing
New York, New York

ISBN 0-671-08726-6

Printed in Hong Kong

CONTENTS

Page 1: Babe Ruth waves his cap to acknowledge fan applause.
Pages 2-3: Pete Rose gets hit number 4191 to tie Ty Cobb's longstanding career hit record.
This page: Mickey Rivers of the New York Yankees steals second.

Top: In the Great Moments Room at the Baseball Hall of Fame in Cooperstown, New York, the sport's greatest moments are recalled through spectacular nine-foot blow-ups. Television monitors feature continuous showings of 'This Week in Baseball.'
Above: Baseball equipment crowds the corner of a dugout.
Left: A cast of Bob Feller's hand grips a baseball autographed by the famous pitcher.
Right: Carlton Fisk and Tom Seaver after Seaver pitched his three hundredth victory.
Far right: Gaylord Perry, overwhelmed by autograph-seekers.

6

INTRODUCTION

Assemble 100 representative American sports fans – people who are knowledgeable and enthusiastic about a whole range of sports – and ask them to name the ten 'greatest moments' in sports. Odds are that a disproportionate number of their nominations will go to baseball. Odds are also that there will be considerable unanimity about at least two dozen of these moments. Almost anyone the least bit aware of sports will nominate Babe Ruth's 'called shot,' Hank Aaron's record setting home run, Joe DiMaggio's hitting streak, or Roger Clemons' 20 strikeouts in one game in 1986.

Why should this be? Why should baseball dominate the market in 'greatest moments?' The answer is probably the subject not of a sports book but of a thick tome on sociology and psychology. Our national pastime does seem to generate a special kind of awareness, a peculiar form of nostalgia.

Consider, for instance, that baseball is one of the few sports that carries its own history around with each game, strapped to its back, so to speak. The anecdotes and statistics of this history are as much a part of the game as are 'peanuts, popcorn, and crackerjacks': listen to the typical television or radio broadcast and you will constantly be reminded of the past moments, trivial as well as great. These statistics are fixed points in time, comprising a sequence of teams and players and games that are always there for points of comparison. Comparisons, furthermore, that fans never seem to tire of hearing again. Fans who

are far too young to have been around on the day a certain player made a 'great hit' or 'great catch' can recount the event as though they had been in the bleachers. Baseball has that effect on people.

But as often as the 'great moments' are recounted, other moments fade. There's no denying that as each decade passes, many of the great moments of the past tend to be replaced by more recent feats. From a practical standpoint, still photos and newsreels from baseball's earlier days cannot hope to compete with the exposure that television affords. It is not surprising that some of the earlier great moments have, in fact, faded completely from memory.

This, then, is a book that defies that fading process, both with moving words and striking photographs. Only the greatest moments of twentieth-century baseball are recounted, not because of any judgment about the quality of the oldtimers' feats, but simply because the game differed in enough ways to make some of their greatest moments unique to their time. But working within this time framework, and restricting ourselves to the major leagues, all the rest of baseball was open to nomination.

While everyone's choices of baseball's most stellar moments must surely differ, the moments captured and memorialized in this book offer a range of players, teams and eras that must never be forgotten. Baseball, the timeless sport in which the action, not a clock, determines its end, offers these moments when time stopped and legends were born.

THE EARLY YEARS

Christy Mathewson pitches three shutouts in the World Series

Perhaps the greatest of all the great pitchers of the first quarter of the twentieth century and still the winningest of all National League pitchers, Christopher Mathewson never won fewer than 22 games a season from 1903 to 1914. In 1908 he won 37 games, still the National League record, and led the league in nine categories including ERA (1.43), strikeouts (259), and shutouts (12). He won 30 games four times, and was the first pitcher in modern baseball to win 30 or more games in three successive seasons.

More than that, he was the most admired player of his time. College-educated, well-mannered and literate at a time when professional baseball was looked upon as a game unfit for women to watch, this 'Galahad among Neanderthals' was the first exemplary baseball hero, a model for parents to point to. As such he played a major role in making baseball a widely accepted national pastime.

Mathewson became a widely-known popular hero after an incredible 1905 World Series performance in which he pitched three shutouts in six days. Pitching for McGraw's Giants during the regular season, he'd logged his third consecutive 30-game year (31-8), and also led the league in ERA (1.27), shutouts

(9) and strikeouts. Interest in the 1905 Series ran particularly high because Mathewson was pitted against the equally brilliant Rube Waddell of Connie Mack's Athletics. The eccentric Waddell had won 26 and lost 11 that year, striking out 286; but the American public was robbed of a great match when a shoulder injury he suffered in horseplay with teammate Andy Coakley forced him to sit out the Series.

In the first game Mathewson faced Eddie Plank and yielded only four hits. He allowed only five other balls to reach the outfield, retiring consecutive Athletic batters for five innings. He also started a rally in the fifth inning that gave the Giants their first two runs (he was third best hitter on his team for the Series), and put the third run of the 3-0 shutout in scoring position with a sacrifice in the ninth.

Philadelphia returned the favor in the second game, Chief Bender shutting out Iron Man McGinnity, 3-0. But in a Series in which all five games were shutouts, these were the last runs the A's would score.

In the third game Mathewson faced Coakley and devastated him, 9-0. As in the first game, Matty gave up only four hits, although this time he walked one man: the A's never got a runner past first base. The only big inning of the Series occurred when the Giants scored five times in the fifth off three hits. No triples or home runs were hit in any of the five games of this best-pitched of all World Series.

Left: The 1905 Giants, with Mathewson as the left inset.
Above: Christy Mathewson warms up his arm. In 1905, the year he pitched his Giants to a world championship, he led the league in wins (31) and ERA (1.27).

The Giants' McGinnity shut out Eddie Plank in the fourth game, 1-0, giving up five hits. Plank gave up four in a disappointing outing in which the single run was unearned. Mathewson faced Chief Bender in the fifth and final game, which remained scoreless through the first four innings. The Giants got on the scoreboard with one run in the fifth, and Mathewson himself scored the final, insurance run after he got on base on a walk in the eighth inning. In the 2-0 shutout Mathewson gave up six hits and retired the last ten batters. The pitching phenomenon had, in his three Series victories, struck out 18 while allowing only 14 hits and one walk.

It was Mathewson's game and Mathewson's Series, but above all it was a pitcher's Series, the victorious Giants batting .203 as a team to the A's abysmal .161. It was also an important win for the National League, which was still smarting from the loss of the first modern Series to the new American League, and from the Giants' refusal to participate in the 1904 Series. But that is another story.

1907

Ty Cobb records his first of nine consecutive American League batting titles

For those who like their heroes larger than life it may come as a shock to learn that Tyrus Raymond Cobb was not born a great natural hitter. Like Babe Ruth, he was one of a kind, and nothing like him has ever been seen before or since on the baseball diamond. In the last forty years only two or three sluggers have hit for a *season* average what Ty Cobb hit for a lifetime batting average – his .367 remains unequaled today. Yet Cobb did so poorly in his first professional outing that he was released by Augusta's Sally League club after 37 games.

The next year, 1905, he did so well with a semi-pro outfit that Augusta called him back, and on 30 August 1905 Ty Cobb put on a Detroit Tigers uniform. In his rookie year he hit only .240. Realizing that he had a problem with low pitches, Cobb went to work. His peerless career, which saw him hit over .320 for 23 years, was a case of mind over matter.

Below: Ty Cobb poses with pitching great Walter Johnson. Cobb took advantage of Johnson's good nature by crowding the plate, knowing Johnson would not throw at him.

Right: Ty Cobb's grip on the bat demonstrates the fact that he was a slap hitter, punching the ball into gaps. *Far right:* Ty Cobb, whose .367 lifetime batting average has never been approached, carefully selects his bat.

In 1906, his first full year in the majors, Cobb signed a $1500-a-year contract and hit .320 in 97 games. By studying individual pitchers' styles and tendencies, Cobb was able to achieve his first great season in 1907. For example, Cobb would crowd the plate with the kind-hearted Walter Johnson pitching, knowing the big man would never throw at him. By the end of the 1907 season Cobb's Tigers had to come up with 14 wins in their last 16 games to win the pennant. Cobb's stellar performance at this time included twice in two games against the New York Highlanders stealing home from first base on sacrifice bunts. Delighting the public and media alike, Cobb was dubbed by the New York *World* the 'Br'er Fox of baseball.' Spirited by Cobb, the Tigers won the pennant. No one could know at the time that Ty Cobb, whose .350 batting average took the batting title, had achieved the first of nine consecutive batting titles (he would take 12 altogether). Cobb's 212 hits and 116 RBI's that year were also league records.

In 1908, the second of three pennant years for the invincible Tigers, Cobb took the American League batting title with a .324 average and again led the league in hits and RBI's, as well as in doubles and triples. The next year, the year of his infamous spiking of Philadelphia's Home Run Baker, he improved, hitting a league-leading .377. Already he was one of the most respected and disliked players the game has ever seen. His behavior in 1910, his fourth consecutive batting title and the first year in four that Detroit did not take the pennant, indicates why and how much.

On the final day of the 1910 season Cobb had a 10-point lead over the great Nap Lajoie. Unwilling to risk the crown, he took himself out of the lineup; Lajoie had to play a doubleheader against the Browns. Out of dislike for Cobb, the Browns' manager and one of his coaches did their best to make it easy for Lajoie who, unaware that anything underhanded was going, took advantage of the rookie they installed on third base and went 8 for 8. Cobb still won, .385 to .384. Those who had tried to help Lajoie were discovered and banished from baseball.

In 1911 Cobb did even better and hit .420; in 1912 he slipped to .410. Cobb next hit .400 in 1922 when he was 37 years old, logging .401 but losing the title to George Sisler with his .420. At the age of 42, in his final major-league season, his twentieth after his first batting title, Cobb hit .323.

How good was he? From his first batting title in 1907 until Babe Ruth and the advent of the lively ball in 1920, baseball was Ty Cobb's game. Quite possibly, his .367 career batting average will never be surpassed. Arrogant, ruthless, intelligent, bigoted, with limitless venom and energy, his skill was so undeniable that in 1936 he received the most votes in the first Hall of Fame election. His manager at Detroit, Hughey Jennings, said that he was the greatest player in history, but that he would trade him if he could get equal value. Equal value was not to be found.

8-16 OCTOBER 1909

Honus Wagner Meets Ty Cobb

Few players in any game really deserve to be called legendary, but as time goes on the career of John Peter Wagner only increases in luster. A hero in his own time, Wagner combined unpretentious good nature with stunning athletic ability, batting over .300 for 17 consecutive years and leading his league in batting eight times (both still National League records). His 722 career stolen bases have been surpassed by only a handful of players in the history of the game, and his fielding, with those famously large hands of his, has been rarely equalled.

Wagner was a player of such stature that he can be mentioned in the same breath only with Ty Cobb and Babe Ruth. Like them, he was one of the first five players drafted into the Hall of Fame, and no one has ever doubted that the Flying Dutchman was one of the greatest shortstops who ever lived. The first man ever to sign him, Edward G Barrow – who also switched Babe Ruth from the pitcher's mound to the outfield – always maintained that Ruth was the game's greatest personality and home run hitter and Cobb was the greatest hitter, but that 'Wagner was the greatest all-round ballplayer who ever lived.' When he died in 1955 at the age of 81, Wagner still led the National League in games played, times at bat, hits, singles, doubles and triples, all records compiled during a 21-year career that ended years before the introduction of the lively ball.

In 1909 Wagner led the league in batting for the fourth straight year (his seventh title), and his Pittsburgh Pirates won the pennant with 110 victories, the highest total in National League history. The Pirates faced American League champions, the Detroit Tigers, in a World Series that would be the first to go seven games. This matchup, one of the most celebrated of the day, pitted the good-natured Wagner against American League batting champion Ty Cobb. Pre-series publicity for the first meeting of Wagner and the ruthless Cobb, a 22-year-old terror, resembled the buildup for a heavyweight boxing match.

Perhaps the fastest as well as the most daring players in their leagues, Cobb and Wagner competed against each other fiercely in this contest which Wagner later dubbed '. . . my finest hour. . . . Cobb stole a total of two bases, I got six; Cobb got six hits, I got eight.' In the first game after slapping a single, Cobb yelled from first base to Wagner, 'Get ready, Krauthead, I'm coming down.' 'I'll be waiting,' replied Wagner, and when Cobb tried to steal, Wagner tagged him so hard with the ball that he split his lip. Cobb taunted Wagner throughout the Series, promising to give him a taste of his spikes when he slid into second. But Cobb learned by the end of the Series that on the field Wagner could be as competitive as anybody.

Wagner and the Pirates took the Series that year, 4-3, Honus leading his team with a batting average of

Above: Honus Wagner, 'The Flying Dutchman,' is considered one of baseball's greatest all-around players.
Page 12: Ty Cobb runs the bases.
Page 13: Honus Wagner played for Pittsburgh for 18 years.

.333 (to Cobb's .231), and stealing six bases to Cobb's two (his six steals stood as a Series record until 1967). Regrettably, this was to be the only time Cobb and Wagner ever faced each other on the field. But fans still had over a decade to debate which of them was the greatest player in baseball before Babe Ruth arrived on the scene to confuse the issue.

3 JULY 1912

Rube Marquard posts his 19th consecutive victory

When Richard William Marquard was purch-ased by the Giants from the American Asso-ciation's Indianapolis team for $11,000 in September of 1908, New York newspapers im-mediately labelled him the '$11,000 Beauty.' His price, exceeding by $1000 the $10,000 paid for Mike Kelly in 1887, was a record for the time, and all the more unprecedented because Marquard was still a minor leaguer, and Kelly had been an established star at time of his purchase.

How much was $11,000? In 1907 Marquard had refused his first major-league offer of $100 a month, from Cleveland, because he was doing better working in an ice cream factory for $25 a week and pitching for the company team.

Marquard, who became known as 'Rube' after the Indianapolis *Star* compared him to pitching great Rube Waddell, was just 18 years old when he came up to the Giants at the end of the 1908 season. He lost his only game that year, and in 1909, with a poor 5-13 record for 29 games, was promptly dubbed the '$11,000 Lemon,' to the embarrassment of team mana-ger John McGraw and the Giant management. He turned in a 4-4 record in 1910, but then, with help from Giant coach Wilbert Robinson, effected a drama-tic turnaround.

In three consecutive years – 1911, 1912 and 1913 (all Giant pennant years) – Marquard's season records were 24-7, 26-11 and 23-10. His 50 wins in the two years 1911 and 1912 made him a New York celebrity (he entered vaudeville and toured off-season as a dance team with his first wife, Blossom Seely), espe-cially because in 1912 Marquard, now the '$11,000 Wonder,' won his first 19 starts. Strictly speaking, his 19 consecutive wins tied the major-league record set by old Giant Tim Keefe in the previous century, but Keefe's record was set when the pitching mound was only 50 feet from the plate.

During Marquard's phenomenal 19-game win-ning streak, which lasted from 11 April through 3 July 1912, he allowed only 49 runs to his opponents, while the Giants scored 139 runs during the same period. He didn't lose a game until 8 July. By then his feat had attracted considerable attention. *The New York Times* of 23 June, at the peak of the streak, devoted a long article to his background and the pro-gress of his record-making. The baseball world was holding its breath as Marquard continued to hurl wins, coming to the mark, on 3 July 1912, that would make history.

Major-league pitchers who have come closest to equalling his 19-win streak include Cleveland's John-ny Allen, who won 15 straight in 1937, and Balti-more's Dave McNally, who won 15 straight in 1969. Christy Mathewson, Carl Hubbell, Ewell Blackwell,

Above: Rube Marquard pitched 19 consecutive wins on his way to a league-leading 26 victories in 1912.
Right: Fred Toney (above) and lefty James Vaughn (below) made history in 1917 with their double no-hitter.

Walter Johnson, Joe Wood, Schoolboy Rowe and Lefty Grove have all put together impressive strings of 16 consecutive wins, but were unable to equal Mar-quard's landmark.

While Rube Marquard, who also won two games in the 1912 World Series, still holds the major-league record for consecutive wins at 19, he himself has pointed out that he would have achieved 20 consecu-tive wins that season under later rules. Entering his twentieth game against Brooklyn, tied up at 3-3 in the eighth inning with the bases loaded, Marquard retired Zack Wheat, Jake Daubert and George Cutshaw in order, and prevented further scoring. The Giants scored the winning run in the bottom of the ninth, but the victory went to starting pitcher Jeff Tesreau. Under current rules, it would have gone to Marquard. Never one to complain, Marquard has been satisfied to see his 19-win streak unduplicated, and was further honored by his induction into the Hall of Fame in 1971, at the age of 81.

Toney and Vaughn pitch a double no-hitter

In the annals of extra-inning no-hitters, the game Frederick Arthur Toney and James Leslie 'Hippo' Vaughn pitched on 2 May 1917 remains unique. The odds against a single pitcher hurling a no-hitter are approximately 500-1; the odds against two pitchers throwing no-hitters in the same game are greater than 250,000-1. But on a cold May day 70 years ago, Fred Toney and Jim Vaughn beat the odds to pitch the only double no-hitter in major-league history.

Both pitchers were big men, both were 29 years old, and both were good pitchers at or near their peaks. Neither Toney's Reds nor Vaughn's Cubs were pennant contenders that year, but Toney turned in a season record of 24-16 with a 2.20 ERA, and Vaughn, who would compile four 20-win seasons and was beginning a four-season stretch in which he would win 85 games and twice lead the league in strikeouts, was 23-13 for 1917, with a 2.01 ERA.

Although he lost, Vaughn threw the better game, just as for his career, he was the better pitcher. The big left-hander's primary weapon was a fastball that earned him a lot of strikeouts. Christy Mathewson, then managing the Cincinnati Reds, started an all right-handed lineup against him but, backed by solid fielding, Vaughn turned in a truly superior game. In the first nine innings he faced the minimum of 27 batters, permitted no runners to get past first, struck out ten, and walked only two. The one ball that did get out of the infield could have been caught.

Toney, who won the game, also walked only two men in the first nine innings. A right-hander without great speed, he relied on a variety of pitches – spitballs, fastballs, curves and fadeaways. He struck out only one man in the first nine innings, and one Cub got to second base, but no Cub got a base hit.

It wasn't until the bottom of the eighth inning that both pitchers realized they were working on no-hitters. Vaughn clinched his no-hitter first, striking out the last two men he faced in the top of the ninth. When Toney retired the side 1-2-3 in the bottom of the ninth, the small crowd, aware that they had witnessed baseball history, cheered both pitchers.

With no score at the top of the tenth, the game continued. The spell was broken when with one out Larry Kopf of the Reds singled off Vaughn. Kopf advanced to third with two out when center fielder Cy Williams dropped a fly ball hit by Hal Chase, and made it home when Indian Jim Thorpe hit a slow ground to Vaughn's left. Vaughn fielded the ball, but catcher Art Wilson froze and blew the play.

Toney retired the Cubs without a hit in the bottom of the tenth, striking out the last two batters he faced to keep his no-hitter going. The win was his, but his name and Vaughn's will always be remembered together for their unique achievement.

THE TWENTIES

1924

Rogers Hornsby hits the highest season average in modern baseball

If Rogers Hornsby wasn't the greatest hitter who ever lived, there is little doubt that he was the best right-handed hitter who ever lived. The 'Rajah' still holds the highest lifetime and single-season batting averages in the National League. Three times in his career he hit .400 or better, a feat equalled only by Ty Cobb and Jesse Burkett (and he hit .397 in 1921). His .358 lifetime batting average is second in major-league history only to Ty Cobb's.

It is said that when he came up to the St Louis Cardinals in 1915, having been purchased from the Western Association's team in Denison, Texas for $400, Hornsby's stance deep in the batters' box,

farther from the plate than any ranking hitter ever stood, with his hands at the very bottom of the bat, disturbed manager Miller Huggins. All efforts to change his stance failed, and Huggins finally gave up, grumbling, 'Well, what do you expect when you pay only $400 for a player?'

With characteristic intransigence, the Rajah kept his peculiar stance. Cold, outspoken and brutally frank, he played on five different teams and managed five different teams in his 23-year career, often quarrelling with owners and fellow players. More than once he was the object of sensational trades and dismissals. But when he picked up a bat, even in batting practice, he commanded attention and respect as have perhaps only two other players – Babe Ruth and Ted Williams.

In 1920 Hornsby took his first of seven batting titles with a .370 average, and in 1921 he began the greatest half-decade of hitting ever known in baseball. From 1920 to 1925 the National League batting crown was his as Hornsby hit .397, .401, .384, .424 and .403, for a five-year average of .402. During these same years he captured the National League home run championship twice, with 42 in 1922 and 39 in 1925, led the league in triples once, and led the league three times in hits, doubles, runs scored and RBI's.

During his unequalled 1924 season, the Rajah was so feared at the plate that pitchers walked him a league-leading 89 times. Together with Hornsby's 227 hits, the walks enabled him to get on base well over half the time that season. Although the .424 batting average he compiled in 1924 is still the highest batting average recorded in the major leagues in the twentieth century, the 1924 MVP award went to Brooklyn hurler Dazzy Vance (28-6). It is an index of just how much Hornsby was disliked as a personality that, despite his brilliant performances of the preceding years (Hornsby was also an excellent fielder), Cincinnati sportswriter Jack Ryder did not even list him among the top ten players of 1924. This omission caused only a mild scandal, and at any rate Hornsby could not be denied the first of his two MVP Awards in 1925.

Left: Rogers 'the Rajah' Hornsby swings the bat. Including his record-making 1924 performance, Hornsby won seven batting titles to end up with an all-time second-place lifetime batting average of .358. He was elected to the Hall of Fame in 1942.
Right: Walter Johnson presents an autographed baseball to Captain Edith Ivings of the Salvation Army.
Right above: Hall of Famer Walter 'the Big Train' Johnson.

10 OCTOBER 1924

Walter Johnson saves the Series for the Senators

Like Rogers Hornsby, the National League's greatest hitter who played in only two World Series, Walter Perry Johnson, probably the fastest pitcher who ever lived, played for a team that rarely allowed him to showcase his talents in postseason play. Johnson pitched for the Washington Senators from 1907 through 1927 and, as the saying went, Washington was 'First in war, first in peace, and last in the American League.'

In 1910 Johnson pitched the first of 10 consecutive seasons in which he won 20 or more games, and won his first of 12 league strikeout titles. In 1923, the second of two consecutive 30-win seasons, he registered an incredible 36-7 win-loss record with a 1.09 ERA and 12 shutouts. His 113 career shutouts are still the record, and his career strikeout mark of 3508 stood until 1983, when Nolan Ryan and Steve Carlton passed it.

But in Johnson's first 13 years, when he was at his best, the Senators finished last twice and seventh five times. Six times Johnson's wins were more than a third of his club's total wins, and six times his wins were more than one quarter of the Senators' wins. As beloved on the mound as Babe Ruth was at bat, the good-natured folk hero compiled his amazing records with consistently mediocre support, a circumstance

that only draws more attention to his great talent. And he did it almost exclusively with one pitch – a ball thrown so fast it could hardly be seen.

It was not until 'The Big Train' was almost 37 years old and nearing the end of his career that the Senators took their first pennant ever. During the 1924 season, his best since his previous 20-win season in 1919, Johnson was 23-7 and led the league in wins, strikeouts, winning percentage, shutouts and ERA, a performance that earned him his second MVP Award. The team the Senators faced in the Series, McGraw's Giants, had just become the first club ever to win four straight pennants, but national attention and sympathy were focused on Walter Johnson's first Series appearance ever.

His first two games were disappointing. In the first game he struck out 12, but also gave up 14 hits, including two homers, to lose in 12 innings, 4-3. In the fifth game, with the Series evened up, his fastball deserted him. 'Boy Wonder' playing manager Bucky Harris kept him in the game when the going got tough – a 'sentimental 'decision for which he was later strongly criticized – and Johnson dropped the game, 6-2. Tears of disappointment were seen in his eyes.

In the seventh and deciding game brilliant maneuvering on the part of manager Harris tricked McGraw into eliminating first baseman Bill Terry – a major batting threat – from the Giant lineup. Washington's left-hander George Mogridge took over from right-hander Curley Ogden after two batters and held the Giants until the sixth inning, when they scored three runs; and right-hander Firpo Marberry prevented any further New York scoring through the eighth inning. Two Washington runs in the bottom of the eighth tied up the score at 3-3.

Walter Perry Johnson and President Calvin Coolidge shake hands at Washington's Griffith Park.

Telling Johnson, 'You're the best we got, Walter. We've got to win or lose with you,' Harris sent his veteran pitcher to the mound at the top of the ninth. All 32,000 spectators at Washington's Griffith Park, including President Calvin Coolidge, rose to their feet to cheer him. With his fastball once again at his command, Johnson struck out five Giants as he held them scoreless for the next four innings. His job was not easy, and he was hit in three innings and walked Hack Wilson in the tenth. Meanwhile New York hurlers Jesse Barnes, Hughie McQuillan and Jack Bentley matched him pitch for pitch, keeping the Senators scoreless and the game tied.

Three big breaks came the Senators' way in the bottom of the twelfth. According to opposing pitcher Bentley, 'Walter Johnson is such a loveable character that the good Lord didn't want to see him beat again.' Giant catcher Hank Gowdy stepped on his own mask chasing a Muddy Ruel pop foul and missed it, affording Ruel the opportunity to double past third. Then Johnson hit an easy grounder to shortstop Travis Jackson, but Jackson fumbled it, leaving two men on base instead of two out. Finally, Earl McNeely hit a ball straight to Freddy Lindstrom. For the second time that day the ball hit a pebble and bounced over Lindstrom's head, giving the slow-moving Ruel time to make it to the plate with the winning run.

Tears came to Johnson's eyes. The Senators had won their first Series ever, and he had won his game.

Grover Cleveland Alexander strikes out Tony Lazzeri and saves the Series

By his own assessment, the most dramatic moment of Grover Cleveland Alexander's dramatic career, the moment he considered the peak of his professional life, occurred in the seventh game of one of the most dramatic Series of all time, the Cardinal/Yankee contest of 1926.

Alexander, who registered 373 lifetime victories, won 30 or more games in three consecutive seasons, and had thrown 16 shutouts in 1916, was already well past his peak in 1926. His battles with alcohol and epilepsy (his drinking may have served to mask his epilepsy, which in those days was less socially acceptable than alcoholism) had taken their toll; besides, he was 39 years old, not young for a pitcher. In fact, after repeated squabbles with manager Joe McCarthy of the Cubs over drinking, Alexander had been let go in June of 1926. Most considered him over the hill. He was believed to pitch best when hungover; he had first entered a sanatorium at the end of the 1925 season.

But when the Cardinals picked him up in midseason Alexander handed manager Rogers Hornsby nine essential victories, and St Louis won its first pennant since 1888. As a reward for their labors, the Redbirds faced a New York club that was studded with players like Babe Ruth and Lou Gehrig.

In the first game Herb Pennock pitched the Yankees to a 2-1 win, but Hornsby, himself as difficult a man as 'Ol' Pete,' did not hesitate to call on his veteran pitcher for the second game. Alexander gave up two runs in the second inning (one was unearned), but then tightened up to retire the last 21 Yankee batters in order, leading St Louis to a 6-2 win. Jesse Haines won the third game for the Cardinals, but the Yankees took the next two. Called upon to pitch the sixth, Alexander evened up the Series, 3-3, with a 10-2 win.

Cardinal ace Jesse Haines was chosen to start against Waite Hoyt in the deciding seventh game, but Hornsby asked Alexander, who had pitched the day before, to warm up two pitchers in the bullpen. The Cardinals were leading 3-2 and Haines pitched well until the seventh inning when, with two men out, he lost control and walked three men to load the bases. It turned out that Haines had developed a blister on his index finger from throwing the knuckleball and was all but unable to throw. The next batter up, rookie Tony 'Poosh 'em Up' Lazzeri, had logged 114 RBI's during the regular season, second in the Yankee lineup only to Babe Ruth.

Alexander, who may or may not have been hungover from celebrating his previous day's victory, had fanned Lazzeri four straight times the day before with his curve ball. He took his time on the mound, letting the younger man 'stew' under the Series pressure.

Lazerri swung on and missed Alexander's first pitch, a curve. But the second pitch, a fastball, was to his liking, and he sent it into the stands with a drive that went foul by only a few feet. Taking notice, Alexander returned to his curve. Lazzeri swung and missed, and the immediate threat to the Cardinals' Series was over.

Alexander then set down the Yankees in order in the eighth. He retired the first two batters in the ninth, then walked Babe Ruth on a three-and-two count. But before he could throw to the next batter, home run hitter Bob Meusel, Ruth inexplicably tried to steal second and was tagged out. The game was over.

'That was the Series and the second big thrill of the day,' said Alexander. 'The third came when Judge Landis mailed out the winners' checks for $5,584.51.' Unfortunately, the rest of Alexander's life was not to be so happy. On the way to a lonely pensioner's grave, he even for a time eked out a living by reciting the tale of the Lazerri strikeout at a Times Square flea market. Curiously enough, Lazzeri was also epileptic, and died at the age of 42 from the effects of a fall caused (it is believed) by an epileptic seizure.

Left: Grover Cleveland Alexander was 39 when he helped the Cardinals to a dramatic Series victory in 1926.
Below: Tony Lazzeri is fanned by Alexander in the seventh inning of the '26 Series with the bases full.

12 OCTOBER 1929

The A's score 10 runs in one inning – the biggest inning in World Series history

After just missing the pennant in 1928, Connie Mack's Philadelphia Athletics breezed to the top of the American League in 1929, finishing 18 games ahead of the second-place Yankees. In the National League, the Cubs took the flag with no greater effort, beating out Pittsburgh by 10 and a half games. Both teams were strong, with rosters that read like future roll calls for the Hall of Fame. The A's featured Al Simmons, Jimmie Foxx, Mickey Cochrane, and hurlers Lefty Grove and George Earnshaw; the Cubs boasted awesome right-handed sluggers Rogers Hornsby, Kiki Cuyler, Hack Wilson and Riggs Stephenson, with hurlers Charlie Root and Pat Malone.

Philadelphia won the first game of the Series, 3-1, behind surprise starter Howard Ehmke, who struck out 13 men (a Series record until 1954). Earnshaw and Grove combined to give Mack his second win, 9-3, but the Cubs' Guy Bush returned the favor in the third game, 3-1. Still, the Cubs had to win the second game at Shibe Park or face the possibility of losing in five.

With Charlie Root pitching like a machine under sparkling blue skies, it looked like the Cubs were going to tie up the Series. They scored two runs in the fourth inning, five in the sixth, and one in the seventh, knocking Jack Quinn, Rube Walberg and Eddie Rommel off the mound. With the Cubs leading 8-0 going into the bottom of the seventh, no one, including Connie Mack, thought the A's had a chance. Mack had in fact already decided that after the regulars had taken their turns at bat, he would substitute en masse, giving even the lowliest scrub the chance to say that he had played in a World Series.

Al Simmons led off for the A's in the bottom of the seventh with a home run. The Athletics felt they had at least been spared the indignity of being shut out. Then Jimmie Foxx, Bing Miller, Jimmy Miller and Joe Boley singled off Root in succession, scoring two more runs. No one felt the outcome was in doubt, but the game was beginning to get interesting.

Pinch hitter George Burns popped up for the first out, but Max Bishop singled to drive in the A's fourth run of the inning. The Cubs' lead had now been cut in half, 8-4. Showing some concern, Chicago manager Joe McCarthy took Root out, choosing southpaw Art Nehf to pitch to the left-handed Mule Haas. Haas socked a burning drive to center, which Hack Wilson lost sight of in the sun. The ball zoomed over Wilson's head and rolled to the 447-foot mark in center field, giving Haas just enough time to slide safely home for an inside-the-park three-run homer. The score was now 8-7, and Philadelphia was back in the game. An exuberant Jimmy Dykes slapped the teammate next to him on the back, sending him flying into the bats. The 'teammate' was none other than Connie Mack him-

self, but with his club only one run down, Mr. Mack was in a forgiving mood.

A thoroughly rattled Art Nehf walked Cochrane, and McCarthy replaced him with Sheriff Blake. Simmons, who had started it all, singled off Blake and then Foxx singled, driving in the tying run. McCarthy brought in the fourth Cub pitcher of the afternoon, Pat Malone, who promptly hit Miller with a pitch to load the bases. Jimmy Dykes then hit a long drive just out of Riggs Stephenson's reach for a double that drove in two runs, and the A's were ahead, 10-8. Malone struck out Boley and Burns to end the inning.

Connie Mack brought in Lefty Grove to protect his two-run lead, and Grove obliged by retiring the Cubs in order in the final two innings, striking out four. Miraculously, the A's had won – they could hardly believe it themselves.

The demoralized Cubs struggled valiantly in the fifth and final game, taking a 2-0 lead into the ninth inning, but once again the A's came from behind and

scored three runs in their final at bat to wrap up the Series. The Philadelphia team that had seen 15 men go to the plate for 10 runs in the greatest rally in World Series history was no fluke, either, as it went on to prove by establishing a dynasty to replace the Yankee dynasty it had annihilated during the regular season, taking the pennant and the world championship again in 1930, and the pennant again in 1931.

Above: Mule Haas slides home on an inside-the-park homer – the seventh of ten runs the A's would score in the seventh inning of the fourth game in the '29 Series.
Above right: Al Simmons started off the seventh-inning A's rally with a home run, then singled later in the inning.
Right: A newspaper account and box score of the amazing game.

ATHLETICS' 10 RUNS IN 7TH DEFEAT CUBS IN 4TH SERIES GAME

Trailing, 8-0, Mackmen Unleash Attack That Beats McCarthy's Men, 10-8, Before 30,000.

15 MEN BAT IN ONE INNING

Four Pitchers, Root, Nehf, Blake and Malone, Used Before Athletics Are Retired.

DYKES'S DOUBLE DECIDES

Simmons, Foxx and Dykes Each Get Two Hits in One Frame—Philadelphians Need One More Game.

By JOHN DREBINGER.

Special to The New York Times.

PHILADELPHIA, Pa., Oct. 12.— Somebody dropped a toy hammer on a stick of dynamite today and touched off an explosion that shook to its heels a continent that Christopher Columbus had discovered 437 they need only one more game to conclude the struggle and win for themselves the lion's share of the spoils.

Never in all world series history was there such an inning. Records, large and small, collapsed in wholesale lots, while a crowd, held speechless for hours, howled itself into a perfect delirium and smashed a few more records.

Root Appeared Out for Revenge.

For six innings the bulky, stolid Charlie Root, whom the fates had treated rather unkindly in the first game in Chicago, appeared riding over the period he had held the mightiest of Mack sluggers in a grip of iron, allowing only three scattered hits and mowing them down as though they were men of straw.

And while Charlie was doing this the Cubs, at last thoroughly aroused, cuffed and battered four of Connie Mack's prized hurlers to all corners of the field. They hammered Jack Quinn, who brought his four-world years and his famed spitball into the fray with high hope, only to carry both out badly shattered. They pulverized Rube Walberg and smashed Ed Rommel.

Charlie Grimm hit a homer, Rogers Hornsby hit a single and a triple, Kiki Cuyler hit three singles in a row, and the 500 loyal rooters from Chicago split their 500 throats. The Philadelphians tried hard to ignore them, but it is difficult to ignore 500 loyal rooters from Chicago.

It was warm and sunny, but the great crowd sulked and sat in silence as Al Simmons stepped to the plate to open the Athletic half of the seventh. Two and three-fifths seconds later the storm broke.

Simmons Collects Homer.

Simmons crashed a home-run on top of the roof of the left-field pavilion. It was Al's second circuit clout of the series and the crowd gave him a liberal hand, though the applause was still lacking in enthusiasm.

"Well," they said, "that at least saves us from a shutout."

But the rumbling continued and in-

Official Box Score of the Fourth World's Series Game

CHICAGO CUBS.

	AB.	R.	H.	TB.	2B.	3B.	HR.	BB.	SO.	SH.	SB.	PO.	A.	E.
McMillan, 3b	4	0	0	0	0	0	0	2	0	0	1	3	0	
English, ss	4	0	0	0	0	0	0	1	1	0	0	2	1	0
Hornsby, 2b	5	2	2	4	0	1	0	0	1	0	0	1	1	0
Wilson, c	3	1	2	2	0	0	0	1	0	0	0	3	0	1
Cuyler, rf	4	2	3	3	0	0	0	1	0	0	0	0	0	1
Stephenson, lf	4	1	1	1	0	0	0	0	0	0	0	2	1	0
Grimm, 1b	4	2	2	5	0	0	1	0	0	0	0	7	0	0
Taylor, c	3	0	0	0	0	0	0	0	1	1	0	8	1	0
Root, p	3	0	0	0	0	0	0	0	1	0	0	0	0	0
Nehf, p	0	0	0	0	0	0	0	0	0	0	0	0	0	0
Blake, p	0	0	0	0	0	0	0	0	0	0	0	0	0	0
Malone, p	0	0	0	0	0	0	0	0	0	0	0	0	0	0
aHartnett	1	0	0	0	0	0	0	0	1	0	0	0	0	0
Carlson, p	0	0	0	0	0	0	0	0	0	0	0	0	1	0
Total	35	8	10	15	0	1	1	3	8	1	0	24	8	2

PHILADELPHIA ATHLETICS.

	AB.	R.	H.	TB.	2B.	3B.	HR.	BB.	SO.	SH.	SB.	PO.	A.	E.
Bishop, 2b	5	1	2	2	0	0	0	0	0	0	0	2	3	0
Haas, cf	4	1	1	4	0	1	0	0	1	0	0	2	0	0
Cochrane, c	4	1	2	3	1	0	0	1	0	0	0	5	0	0
Simmons, lf	5	2	2	5	0	0	1	0	2	0	0	0	0	0
Foxx, 1b	4	2	2	2	0	0	0	0	0	0	0	10	0	0
Miller, rf	3	1	2	2	0	0	0	0	0	0	0	3	0	1
Dykes, 3b	4	1	5	4	1	0	0	0	0	0	0	2	0	0
Boley, ss	3	1	1	1	0	0	0	0	1	1	0	1	5	0
Quinn, p	2	0	0	0	0	0	0	0	2	0	0	0	0	0
Walberg, p	0	0	0	0	0	0	0	0	0	0	0	0	0	1
Rommel, p	0	0	0	0	0	0	0	0	0	0	0	0	0	0
bBurns	2	0	0	0	0	0	0	0	1	0	0	0	0	0
Grove, p	0	0	0	0	0	0	0	0	0	0	0	0	0	0
Total	36	10	15	23	2	0	2	1	6	2	0	27	10	2

a Batted for Malone in the eighth.
b Batted for Rommel in the seventh.

SCORE BY INNINGS.

Chicago	0	0	0	2	0	5	1	0	0— 8
Philadelphia	0	0	0	0	0	0	10	0	x—10

THE THIRTIES

1930

Hack Wilson sets National League records of 190 RBI's and 56 home runs

Lewis Robert 'Hack' Wilson, 195 pounds of slugger on a five-foot-six frame, was an instant favorite with Giant fans when John McGraw brought him up in 1924. McGraw had great faith in his future, but a clerical error exposed Wilson to the draft, enabling Joe McCarthy to snap him up in 1925 for $5000, one of the great bargains in baseball history. McCarthy observed, 'I wouldn't trade him for any other outfielder in baseball. He can hit, run, and throw.'

It was during his years with McCarthy's Cubs that Hack became a full-fledged folk hero. He was called 'Hack' after the Cubs' Hack Miller, built somewhat like him, who was called 'Hack' after a popular Russian wrestler of the day named Hackenschmidt. From 1926 through 1930 Wilson led the National League in homers four times, logged more RBI's than anyone except Babe Ruth and Lou Gehrig and, as the National League's foremost slugger, received the highest salary in the game after Ruth. Bordering on the irresponsible, Wilson had little respect for training rules and curfews, but he liked McCarthy and the Cubs. He definitely liked a drink, and became intimate with much of the population of Chicago after hours.

In 1926 he led the National League in home runs with 21, batted .321, and logged 109 RBI's. He followed up his performance in 1927 with a league-leading 30 homers, batting .318 and logging 129 RBI's, and in 1928 he led with 31, batted .313, and logged 120 RBI's. Hack helped his Cubs to the Series in 1929 with 39 homers (second only to Chuck Klein's new league record of 43), 156 RBI's (a new league record), and a .345 average, but he was only warming up for his incomparable 1930 season. That year Wilson came into his own with 208 hits – 35 of them doubles, 6 of them triples and 56 of them home runs – scored 146 runs, belted in 190 runs, and hit for a .356 average (he also led the league in walks and strikeouts, and registered 423 total bases with an awesome .723 slugging percentage). His 56 homers are still the National League record, and his 190 RBI's are the major-league record.

Historians like to point out that 1930 was the year of the juiced-up ball, but everyone was hitting the same ball, and even if averages were inflated, no one else did what Wilson did. His 56 homers have of course been bettered in the American League and can't stand forever, but his 190 RBI's, like Gehrig's 2130 consecutive games, appears to be as impregnable as any record can be. Gehrig had 184 RBI's in 1931 and Hank Greenberg had 183 in 1937, but since then no one has even come close, and season highs have fallen off sharply. Medwick's 154 in 1937 and Tommy Davis's 153 in 1962 appear to be more representative of top possible figures.

At the end of the 1930 season Rogers Hornsby replaced Joe McCarthy as the Cubs' manager. Wilson, who needed plenty of space, feuded with Hornsby over conditioning. Claiming 'He's ruining my career,' in 1931 he hit only 13 homers and batted in only 61 runs, and at the end of the 1932 season he was traded to the Dodgers. Two years after he had commanded a Depression salary of $33,000, he was out of baseball and on the streets. One of the greatest sluggers the National League has ever seen, Wilson died penniless at the age of 48 in 1948. A special grant of $350 from the National League saved him from a pauper's grave. His reputation for drinking and fighting, as well as his relatively brief reign of greatness, kept him out of the Hall of Fame until 1979.

Left: Cubs slugger Hack Wilson poses with his bat.
Above: Hall of Famer Hack Wilson hits during practice.
Below: Babe Ruth, photographed in 1932.

Babe Ruth's 'Called Shot'

On 1 October 1932, Babe Ruth, in his tenth and last World Series performance, hit a home run off Cubs' pitcher Charley Root in the fifth inning of the third game of the Yankees-Cubs Series. His fifteenth and last World Series homer, it broke the game's 4-4 deadlock and helped the Yankees take their third straight game of the Series as they slugged their way to their third consecutive Series sweep.

Legend has it that The Bambino, in 'one of the more brazen and defiant gestures of all baseball history,' pointed to where he was going to hit this home run. Although not one reporter covering the game that day included it in his story, according to a no less impeachable source than 'The Sporting News' *Official World Series Records,* 'Ruth . . . pointed to the most distant part of Wrigley Field, took two deliberate strikes, and then hit a homer to the bleacher to which he had pointed.'

But did he really 'call' his homer? Was he merely pointing to the Cubs' dugout to silence hecklers? Did

23

he even point at anything at all? The Bambino himself never clarified the question, equivocating, when pressed, with such statements as, 'I didn't exactly point to any spot, like the flagpole. Anyway, I didn't mean to. I just sort of waved at the whole fence. . . .' The truth may lie somewhere between fanciful thinking and reality.

There was a lot of bitter feeling between the clubs in the 1932 World Series. First of all, Joe McCarthy, in his second season of managing the Yankees, had been fired as manager of the Cubs by owner William Wrigley in the last week of the 1930 season. Just as significant was the presence on the Chicago team of former Yankee star Mark Koenig. Koenig had been added to

the Cubs late in the season, and although he had been instrumental in Chicago's pennant-winning spurt, he was voted only half a share of World Series earnings by his new club. The Yankees were outraged by this lack of respect, and accused the Cubs of cheapness; the Cubs knew how to give as well as take. 'Balloon Head' and 'Big Belly' were two of the printable insults they hurled at Babe Ruth.

The Cubs were riding him mercilessly when he came to bat in that fateful fifth inning. Showman that he was, he held up one finger after the first strike. He held up two fingers after the second strike. Everyone saw that. Then, according to some, he pointed to a spot in center field. This 'point' may have been his hand coming down after his 'strike two' gesture; he may have been indicating that he had one strike left (that is what catcher Gabby Hartnett claimed he heard him say). The Bambino, apparently unwilling to impede the growth of his legend in the twilight of his career, later conceded that he had 'waved' to the fence, but manager Joe McCarthy didn't see any gesture, pitcher Root didn't see any gesture, and not one reporter in the park that day reported such a gesture in his column. Eye-witness Damon Runyon didn't mention it in his front-page story which appeared the next day. The first printed mention of a 'called homer' appeared at least three days after the game. The account that the Babe first called his shot and then deliberately let two strikes go by took years to make it into ink. Perhaps the truth may never be known, but whether or not one of the greatest moments in baseball history ever happened, the story imparts another glimmer of glory to the legend that is Babe Ruth.

---

10 JULY 1934

Carl Hubbell's amazing All-Star game performance

So important during his 16-year career with the New York Giants that he was known as 'The Meal Ticket,' left-hander Carl Owen Hubbell owed his dominance to a single pitch, a screwball which he perfected into one of the most potent weapons the game has ever seen. Blended with his dazzling change of pace, the screwball began to pay off for Hubbell in 1933 when he won a league-leading 23 games, including 10 shutouts, a 1.66 ERA and 309 innings pitched – all league records. The 1933 season was also his first of five consecutive 20-game years, and the first of his three MVP years. Three years later Hubbell would achieve an all-time record of 24 consecutive wins over the 1936 and 1937 seasons, pulling his career high of 26-8 in 1936.

In 1933, from 13 July to 1 August, King Carl logged 46 consecutive innings of shutout pitching. Personally, Hubbell considers his greatest single performance to be his 18-inning shutout of the Cardinals on 2 July 1933. In that game he struck out 12, allowed only six hits, gave up no walks, and beat out a double-play grounder to keep the eighteenth inning alive and

Left: Commissioned by Chevrolet, the painting by Robert Thom of Babe Ruth's 'called shot' was presented, at the 1976 All-Star game, to Commissioner Bowie Kuhn, who donated it to the Hall of Fame.
Below: Action shots depict Carl Hubbell's delivery.

11 & 15 JUNE 1938

Johnny Vander Meer's back-to-back no-hitters

Unique among one-time records is John Samuel Vander Meer's remarkable back-to-back no-hitters. Up to the time he set it only two pitchers had ever recorded two no-hitters in a career, and none had ever logged two in the same season. Nowadays, of course, whenever a pitcher throws a no-hitter everyone watches his next start anxiously to see if he will equal Vander Meer's feat; but before Vander Meer, it is probable that no pitcher even considered back-to-back no-hitters a possibility.

Vander Meer himself, now in his late sixties, sagely notes that 'Records of all types are inevitably broken.' But in this case he may be wrong. If baseball is played long enough, another pitcher may duplicate his back-to-back no-hitters; but it would take a superhuman pitcher with supernatural luck to set a new record of three consecutive no-hitters.

Above left: Lou Gehrig, fanned by Hubbell, at practice.
Below: Vander Meer's no-hit streak finally ends.

ensure the Giant win. But as far as baseball fans are concerned, his most memorable outing occurred the following season (he was 21-12 with a league-leading 2.30 ERA in 1934) when he was lead-off National League pitcher at the second All-Star game.

When Hubbell showed up at the Polo Grounds on 10 July 1934 he faced an American League starting lineup of Charlie Gehringer, Heinie Manush, Babe Ruth, Lou Gehrig, Jimmie Foxx, Al Simmons, Joe Cronin, Bill Dickey and Lefty Gomez, all now in the Hall of Fame.

Gehringer led off with a single to center on Hubbell's first pitch, taking it to second when Wally Berger mishandled the ball. Hubbell walked Heinie Manush, and with two men on and no outs found himself facing Babe Ruth, Lou Gehrig and Jimmie Foxx. As Babe Ruth came to the plate, catcher Gabby Hartnett called time, jogged out to Hubbell, and told him to use his screwball, saying it always got Ruth out. Apparently Hubbell took his advice.

Babe Ruth took one ball and swung at and missed three straight screwballs. Lou Gehrig also took one ball and went down swinging at three straight screwballs. Jimmie Foxx actually foul-tipped one of the three screwballs he missed, and the inning was over.

At the top of the second inning Hubbell struck out Al Simmons, who would hit .344 that season, again using his screwball. The crowd went wild. Then he fanned Joe Cronin for his fifth consecutive strikeout against five of the best hitters ever to bat in succession in one game. Bill Dickey singled off him, but Hubbell fanned Lefty Gomez to crown his performance – six strikeouts in two innings.

Hubbell, a gifted comedian who did as well on the rubber chicken circuit as he did on the mound, boasted about having struck out in such distinguished hitting company; but American League All-Star captain Joe Cronin said it best: 'Hubbell . . . had something no other pitcher has – a screwball, with which you can't do a thing.'

Johnny Vander Meer demonstrates his powerful wind-up.

Like many promising young pitchers with speed, Vander Meer was wild. His lack of control almost cost him his chance in the majors, and he bounced from Brooklyn to Cincinnati to Boston before ending up again at Cincinnati at the end of 1937, where manager Bill McKechnie helped him alter his delivery slightly. In 1938 Vander Meer won five of his first seven games on the way to a 15-10 record in his first full major-league season.

His first no-hitter, on 11 June, was a more artistic game than his second. He retired the first nine Boston batters in the game and, after momentary loss of control of his fastball, retired the last 13 as well, fanning four. He faced only 28 men, and the three who got on base did so on walks. None got past first base. His team was solid behind him in the 3-0 victory. Ernie Lombardi in particular contributed with a two-run homer, and turned in some excellent fielding.

Opening four days later against Brooklyn (both teams he blanked had previously rejected him), Vander Meer also made history by starting in the first night game in New York City. Brooklyn general manager Larry MacPhail had arranged special festivities for the occasion, and the game, with 40,000 in attendance, did not get underway until 9:45. Vander Meer's wildness showed that evening, and he walked eight men, striking out seven.

In the fourth inning the Reds scored four runs, adding two more in the ninth, giving Vander Meer a comfortable 6-0 lead. He suffered from wildness in the seventh, walking two men before he regained control; but he retired the Dodgers in order in the eighth, striking out two.

He got Buddy Hassett to ground out on his first pitch in the ninth. Then once again his control deserted him, and he walked Babe Phelps, Cookie Lavagetto and Dolf Camilli to load the bases. Manager McKechnie came out to calm him down: 'Take it easy, Johnny, but get the no-hitter.'

Vander Meer got Ernie Koy to ground to Lou Riggs, who threw to home for the force out. There was only one more out to go, but the bases were still loaded. By now even the Dodger fans at Ebbets Field were rooting for Vander Meer's no-hitter. The tension was unbearable.

Next up was Leo Durocher. He hit a long foul, then popped up into short center field. It was an easy catch for Harry Craft, and Vander Meer entered baseball legend. Although his subsequent career was an anticlimax and there is a temptation to dismiss him as a fluke, Vander Meer pitched another three and one-third scoreless innings in his next game to set a National League record of 21 and one-third consecutive scoreless innings, and he won nine games in a row that year before he was beaten. Arm problems, following immediately after his 1938 season and continuing throughout his career, contributed more than anything else to limiting him to a career which showed great promise, rather than one which was consistently outstanding.

Gabby Hartnett's 'homer in the gloamin'

The Pirates were so certain that they would be playing in the 1938 World Series that they built a new press box at Forbes Field. All that remained, apparently, was for the Bucs, who led Chicago by a game and a half, to win once from the Cubs in a three game series to be held at Wrigley Field.

But to everyone's surprise, the sore-armed Dizzy Dean, who had been purchased from the Cardinals for three players and $185,000 that April, came through for the Cubs and handed them a 2-1 victory. The Cubs were now only a half game out of tying for first place in the National League, and the stage was set for one of the most dramatic moments in pennant race history.

It was a dark afternoon on that 28 September when Clay Bryant started for Chicago and Bob Klinger started for Pittsburgh. As the lead seesawed back and forth, a total of nine pitchers trudged to the mound. In the top of the eighth inning, the Pirates finally took the lead, 5-3, but the Cubs came back in the bottom of the eighth, adding two more runs before they were stopped by fireman Mace Brown and a brilliant defensive play by right fielder Paul Waner, whose masterful throw cut down the tie-breaking run at the plate.

Darkness was descending and it was getting hard to see, but the umpires decided to let the teams play one more inning. If the score remained tied, a replay would be scheduled for the next day, an eventuality that would be of distinct disadvantage to the Cubs, whose pitching staff was worn out.

Chicago's Charlie Root retired the Pirates with no trouble in the top of the ninth. Then Mace Brown put out the first two Cubs he faced. Next up was Charles Leo 'Gabby' Hartnett, a veteran catcher who had replaced Charlie Grimm as the Cubs' manager in mid-season. Old Tomato Face swung at Brown's first pitch and missed. He barely tipped the second pitch, but on the next one, a fastball Brown hoped would end the game, Hartnett, barely able to see in the bad light, connected for a booming home run, a roundtripper that soon become immortalized as his 'homer in the gloamin'.'

By the time he reached second base there were so many players and fans on the field that he couldn't see the bag. 'I don't think I walked a step to the plate,' he later said. 'I was carried in.'

The Pirates were so demoralized by this loss that the fight went out of them, and they dropped the third straight game of the series, 10-1. Fired up by their win, the Cubs went on to take the National League pennant, continuing a three-year schedule which saw them take flags in 1929, 1932, 1935 and 1938.

Above right: Gabby Hartnett is greeted at home plate by exuberant teammates after his game-winning homer.
Right: Lou Gehrig, benched after 2130 consecutive games.

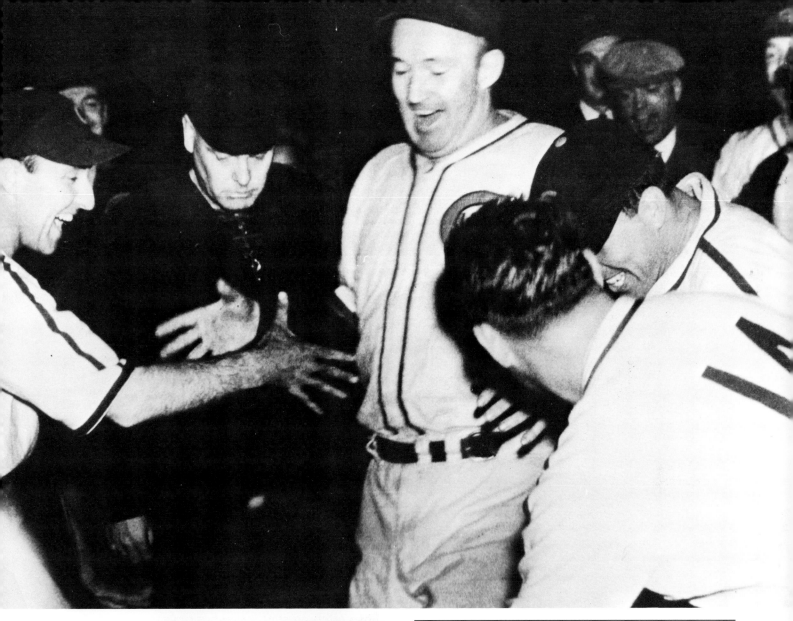

2 MAY 1939

Lou Gehrig takes himself out of the lineup after 2130 consecutive games played

On 2 June 1925 veteran Yankee first baseman Wally Pipp was hit in the side of the head during batting practice and complained of a headache. Manager Miller Huggins told him to take the day off and started young Lou Gehrig at his position. Pipp never played another game for the Yankees. But for the next 14 years Lou Gehrig did not once fail to appear in the Yankee lineup, and thereby amassed the all-time endurance record of 2130 consecutive games played. (Gehrig's 2130 consecutive games in fact began the day before, 1 June, when he pinch hit for Pee Wee Wanninger.)

During his 14 years as a Yankee Gehrig built a reputation for stamina and dependability that earned him such nicknames as 'The Iron Horse' and 'the Pride of the Yankees.' Batting and throwing left-handed, he logged 493 home runs and a healthy .340 lifetime batting average; his 10 World Series homers are a tribute to his usually outstanding October play. He led the league in RBI's five times, in home runs three

times, and was named MVP three times. Gehrig took the American League batting title with a .363 average in 1934 (his high was .379 in 1930), five times hit over 40 home runs, hit 23 grand slam homers (an all-time record), and got more than 40 doubles seven times and 10 or more triples eight times.

Even after he was beaned so badly that many thought his skull was fractured and his streak was over, Gehrig bounced right back, banging out three triples the next day. On 13 July 1934 what was diagnosed as lumbago forced him to be led off the field in the first inning. With his streak standing at 1426, Gehrig appeared in one at bat at the top of the order the next day, despite excruciating pain, to preserve his record. He singled and was replaced by a pinch runner.

But something was clearly wrong by the end of the 1938 season. The Iron Horse's 1938 Series performance was strangely lackluster, and at spring training the following year his efforts to swing a bat and field were appallingly pathetic. Gehrig knew he was through in his eighth and final game of the 1939 season when his teammates praised him after he

didn't bungle a routine out. 'They meant it to be kind,' he said, 'but it hurt worse than any bawling out I ever got in baseball.' He was batting a sub-standard .143 for the season.

His reflexes were so shot that manager Joe McCarthy feared for his safety, but the great Yankee manager could not bring himself to ask Gehrig to step down. On 30 April 1939, Lou Gehrig, then team captain and the highest-paid player in baseball, asked McCarthy to take him out of the lineup for the next game. He was 36 years old.

On 2 May 1939 at a Yankee-Tiger game, the Pride of the Yankees, for the first time ever, handed out a lineup card with his name left off. When the announcement was made that he had voluntarily taken himself out of the lineup, the Detroit fans gave him a huge ovation; Gehrig doffed his cap and sat down, perhaps thinking he would be able to return after a rest, probably unaware that he had played his last game. Two years later, two weeks short of his thirty-eighth birthday, he died from the muscle-wasting amyotrophic lateral sclerosis, a degenerative disease so rare it was named after him.

THE FORTIES

Bob Feller pitches a no-hitter on opening day

Bob Feller, the only genuine prodigy in baseball history, began pitching in the big leagues at the age of 17, and in a career interrupted by four years in the Navy, led the American League in strikeouts seven times. Among his other records, 'Rapid Robert' logged 12 one-hitters, more than twice as many as any other pitcher has ever been able to achieve. His fastball was clocked at upwards of 98.6 miles per hour.

Feller pitched three no-hitters in his career, a mark that has since been passed by Sandy Koufax and Nolan Ryan, but one of his no-hitters seems destined to remain unique in baseball history forever. Most pitchers take some time to get going, and it is unlikely that anyone will ever duplicate Feller's feat of throwing a no-hitter on opening day.

It was a raw, blustery day in Chicago on 16 April 1940 when Feller took the mound for the Cleveland Indians against the Chicago White Sox. The year before he had logged his first 20-win major-league season, leading the American League with a 24-9 record and 246 strikeouts; this year he would do even better – 27-11, with 261 strikeouts. But on opening day of 1940, at the age of 21, he did not feel he had his best stuff. Although he managed to keep the White Sox hitless and scoreless, he was still struggling with his youthful wildness, and he walked four men in the first two innings.

In the top of the third inning the Indians scored a run. With something to protect, Feller began tightening up his game. From the third into the ninth inning, he retired 20 White Sox batters in a row. Feller had excellent support from Ben Chapman, who made some fine catches in right field, from Ken Keltner at third, and especially from Ray Mack at second, whose tough play in the eighth, scooping up a slow roller off pinch hitter Larry Rosenthal and making an off-balance throw to first, undoubtedly saved the no-hitter.

Above left: Lou Gehrig is touched by the ovation given him by 75,000 fans gathered at Yankee Stadium to honor him on 4 July 1939.
Right: Hall of Famer Bob 'Rapid Robert' Feller pitched for Cleveland for his entire 18-year career.

Above: The batter is still swinging after the ball has popped out of Hemsley's glove during Feller's opening day no-hitter.
Right: Floyd Giebell pitched a crucial shutout against Feller.
Far right: The 1940 pennant-winning Detroit Tigers.

By the seventh inning the Cleveland team knew they were working on a no-hitter. The dugout was unusually quiet. When Feller went out for the bottom of the ninth his game was still intact, but the score was only 1-0, Indians, and he was under no illusions. 'I knew I had a chance for a no-hitter, but I tried to put the thought out of my mind by reminding myself you never have a no-hitter until the last man is out. I got to thinking I'd just pitch my own ball game. A pitcher can't be any better than he is.'

He retired the first two batters, then faced Luke Appling, a 20-year veteran who had hit over .300 for six straight seasons (.388 in 1936) and seldom struck out. The count went to three-and-two. Appling fouled off four pitches, and finally, on the tenth pitch, Feller walked him.

Taft Wright, up next, slashed a grounder that looked like a hit, but Ray Mack knocked it down and threw him out. The opening day no-hitter was Feller's. Neither he nor his catcher, Rollie Hemsley, felt it was his best game, but the victory was particularly sweet because Feller's sister, his mother and his father – who had started him playing baseball before he could walk – had all been present to see him pitch his first no-hitter.

27 SEPTEMBER 1940

Floyd Giebell shuts out Bob Feller to save the pennant for the Tigers

The Detroit Tigers came into the final week of the 1940 season deadlocked with Cleveland and New York for first place in the American League. With three days of the schedule left, they needed a victory over Cleveland and a Yankee loss to the Philadelphia Athletics to clinch the pennant. All their starting pitchers were arm-weary. Tiger manager Del Baker called a meeting before the essential game to explain the situation to the players.

Regulars Bobo Newsom (21-5), Schoolboy Rowe (16-3) and Tommy Bridges (12-9) volunteered to start, but Baker had a different idea. He asked his players to approve Floyd George Giebell to go up against Bob Feller, who with 27 wins was having his best season ever. Giebell, a 25-year-old right-hander, had pitched 15 and a third innings for Detroit in 1939, winning one game and losing one game. In 1940, after spending most of the year down on the farm with the International League's Buffalo club, he had been recalled by the Tigers in the last two weeks of the season, and had played and won one game. The players approved Baker's choice.

Giebell, with poise and confidence, kept pace with Feller through three scoreless innings, and re-fused to become upset even when wild partisan Indian fans threw rubbish at Hank Greenberg and hit Tiger catcher Birdie Tebbetts with a quantity of garbage so great that Tebbetts had to be helped from the field.

In the fourth inning the Tigers scored the only runs of the day when Charlie Gehringer walked, Greenberg fanned and Rudy York slashed his thirty-third home run of the season into the left-field seats. In Cleveland's fourth, Roy Bell and Kenny Keltner singled, but Giebell put a stop to the rally when he struck out Ray Mack.

In the seventh inning Giebell had to defend himself again when a single by Mack, an error by Gehringer and a sacrifice by Feller put Indian runners on first and third with one out. Giebell rose to the occasion, fanning Ben Chapman and retiring Roy Weatherly on a routine grounder, and went on to retire the last six batters in order to win the game and clinch the pennant for the Tigers.

Giebell allowed six hits to Feller's three in his game. He walked two and struck out six, but was not eligible to appear in the World series. He played only 34 and a third innings for the Tigers the following year, with no wins or losses and, after a total of 67 and two-thirds innings pitched during three years with the Tigers (for a career record of 3-1), dropped out of baseball and out of sight forever. Only his timely performance against Bob Feller reminds us of his name.

Joe DiMaggio's all-time record 56-game hitting steak comes to an end

While Nazi Luftwaffe battered London on 15 May 1941, the Chicago White Sox battered the New York Yankees, 13-1. In the first inning of this game the great Joe DiMaggio made a memorable bad throw which hit a baserunner; he also got a hit. This single – which drove in the only Yankee run – seemed unremarkable at the time, but it marked the beginning of the greatest hitting streak ever recorded in the history of baseball.

Joseph Paul DiMaggio would go on to get hits in 56 consecutive games (he also hit safely in the All-Star game). Many experts, including Ted Williams, feel that his feat is the greatest single accomplishment in baseball history, dwarfing home run records, season average and RBI records, and even record pitching feats. While compiling his record, DiMaggio also helped lift the Yankees from fourth place to capture the flag on 4 September, the earliest pennant-clinching date in history.

By 1 June DiMaggio's streak stood at 18, nothing extraordinary. On 2 June, the day Lou Gehrig died, he singled and doubled off Bob Feller to make it 19. On 8 June, when he broke his personal 23-game record, DiMaggio himself began to take notice. By 10 June, when he had hit in 25 consecutive games, the nation began to take notice.

Bob Feller failed to stop him on 14 June; at 26 games, DiMaggio passed Babe Ruth's record. On 17 June, when the streak moved to 30, the news programs of a nation on the brink of world war were interrupted with, 'The streak is alive!' Joe DiMaggio, one of the most private of persons, became the most talked-about athlete in America.

On 21 June his streak stood at 34, bettering Rogers Hornsby's National League record of 33. On 28 June pitcher Joe Babich of Philadelphia vowed to stop DiMaggio from making the streak 40, even if it meant

Left: On his way to a record, DiMaggio bats in the forty-second consecutive game in which he logged a hit. *Above:* DiMaggio keeps his streak alive, connecting for a hit during a doubleheader against the Red Sox on 1 July at Yankee Stadium.

giving him nothing to hit. DiMaggio responded by hitting a bad ball through Babich's legs for a double. The next day, at a doubleheader in Washington, he tied and broke George Sisler's American League record of 41 games.

Only one standing record was left, and on 2 July, playing against his brother Dom of the Red Sox, Joe DiMaggio blasted one of 15 homers he would hit during the streak to bring the record to 45 consecutive games, topping Wee Willie Keeler's record of 44 set in 1897.

With the pressure off, DiMaggio got even hotter: in the streak's final 10 games he got 23 hits in 40 times at bat (a .575 average). The end came on 17 July 1941 at Cleveland's Municipal Stadium where 67,468 fans,

the largest night game attendance to date, had come to see what he would do. His first two at bats resulted in sharply hit shots over third base which Ken Keltner, back-handing them both, somehow managed to catch. Then DiMaggio walked, and finally, facing hurler Jim Bagby, he hit a hot one to shortstop Lou Boudreau, who turned it into a double play. The streak was over.

DiMaggio immediately began a new streak, and hit in his next 17 consecutive games. For a season in which he struck out only 13 times in 541 trips to the plate, DiMaggio hit 30 home runs and got 125 RBI's, with a .357 batting average. No one has come near his 56 consecutive games since, and many experts still agree with Ted Williams that his 1941 performance is a record 'that will never be changed.'

1941

Ted Williams breaks .400 on the last day of the season

It is no accident that Theodore Samuel Williams – hot-tempered, arrogant, opinionated and antagonistic – was the best offensive player in modern baseball. Hitting was his life. He had devoted most of his waking hours to mastering his art since he was a child, giving it the attention scientists presumably give to their life work. 'I was a guy,' Williams said, 'who practiced until the blisters bled. And then I practiced some more.'

And then there was his eye. Williams said that he could follow the ball from the moment it left the pitcher's hand until the moment it crossed the plate, a claim born out by his 2018 career walks (opposed to 2654 hits), second only to Babe Ruth, and his mere 709 career strikeouts. Only three times in 19 years of major-league play did he strike out more than 50 times in a season. He avoided beanballs by flicking his head rather than hitting the dirt. Casey Stengel once remarked, 'I bet there wasn't more than a dozen times in his life that he was really fooled by a pitch.'

As a rookie in 1939, Williams led the American League with 145 RBI's, hit 31 homers, batted .327, and was second in walks with 107, the most walks ever for a rookie. But it was in 1941, when he was 23 years old and still learning, that Williams became the first major-leaguer since 1930 to break .400. So far, he is still the last major-leaguer to hit .400, and his .406 in 1941 remains the highest single-season batting average since Rogers Hornsby's .424 in 1924.

Williams set his mark in a dramatic style all his own. Beginning the year with a chipped ankle, he got off to a slow start, but soon fell into a groove. His average for June was .436. It was still over .400 around All-Star time, and he pushed it up to .402 by the end of August. His average for September was .413, and with one week left in the season, he was batting .406.

When Red Sox manager Joe Cronin suggested he sit out the remaining games to protect his average, Williams replied, 'If I'm a .400 hitter, I'm a .400 hitter for the entire season, not a part of one. I'll play out the year.'

Going into the final day of the season, a doubleheader against the Athletics, Williams was batting .3995 – a flat .400. Still refusing to sit down, he got a hit his first time at bat, and went 4-for-5 in the first game, collecting three singles and a home run. In the second game, he singled and doubled in three times at bat. The season was over now, and Ted Williams had averaged .406. Joe DiMaggio took MVP honors that year behind his awesome 56-game hitting streak, and Williams had to wait until 1946 to collect his first MVP, largely because some voters couldn't abide his personality. But regardless of what anybody might think, Ted Williams' .406 batting average in 1941 is a record that nobody can take away. At least so far, nobody has.

Above: Ted Williams awaits his turn at batting practice.
Below: Ted Williams belts a triple on 11 August 1941, on his way to a .406 season batting average.
Right: Bill Dickey crosses the plate after his two-run homer that clinched the Series for the Yankees.
Below right: Bill Dickey fields a foul ball.

Bill Dickey's two-run homer clinches the Series for the Yankees

In 1943 the major leagues were seriously feeling the effects of World War II. The Yankees had lost Johnny Sturm and Tommy Henrich to the armed forces in 1942. In 1943 they lost Joe DiMaggio, Phil Rizzuto, Red Ruffing and Buddy Hassett. Other teams lost players too, but it came as no surprise to anyone that the Yankees and the Cardinals – both teams with extensive farm systems – again dominated their leagues and faced each other in the World Series for the second straight year. Both clubs had breezed to their 1943 league titles, the Cardinals finishing 18 games ahead of the second-place Reds, the Yankees outdistancing Washington by 13 and a half games.

In the 1942 Series the Cardinals, hot off an incredible end-of-season streak, had dropped the first game but returned to take the next four games straight, upsetting the seemingly invincible Yankees, who had won their last eight consecutive World Series contests. The Yankees were looking for revenge against the Redbirds in 1943, but were weakened by the loss of some of their most able veterans. The Cardinals, staffed by a seemingly endless supply of fast, young, underpaid players from Branch Rickey's farm system, seemed poised to repeat their stirring 1942 Series victory. History was to show that the Cardinals had reached their peak in 1942, but as the 1943 Series opened, it was anybody's contest.

Just as in the 1942 Series, the Cards lost the first game but, spirited by the pitching and catching Cooper brothers, Mort and Walker (whose father had died that morning) they took the second game, 4-3. History did not repeat itself further, however, for the Cardinals lost the third game, 6-2, after holding a 2-1 lead into the eighth inning; they went on to drop the next two games, in which they scored a total of only one run.

The highlight of the fifth and deciding game in this dramatic Series came in the sixth inning. Pitching for the Cardinals, Mort Cooper fanned the first two batters who faced him, but received little support from his teammates, who left altogether 11 men stranded on base without scoring. Pitching for the Yankees, Spud Chandler had no more support, and both teams were scoreless going into the sixth. Then New York's Charlie Keller got on base and Bill Dickey, whose .362 average in 1936 is still the major-league record for a catcher, smashed a home run that broke the ice, giving the Yankees the game, 2-0, and the Series. For New York, this was their tenth world championship, their seventh under manager Joe McCarthy. Although the Cardinals' hopes of repeating that year were dashed, they returned to take the Series in 1944 from their hometown rivals, the St Louis Browns, who had won their first pennant ever – from the Yankees – on the last day of the season.

Cookie Lavagetto's ninth-inning double stymies the Yankees

Dodgers-Yankees 'subway Series' always attracted considerable attention, and the Brooklyn-Manhattan clash of 1947, the first of six such Series in the ten years between 1947 and 1956, was no exception. Could the lowly Brooklyn Bums, champions of proletariat America, overcome the might Yankees, baseball aristocrats, the image of dignity, class and refinement? The Dodgers-Yankees Series of these years were more than a baseball rivalry, they were the stuff of myth.

The 1947 Series stood out for more reasons than the special drama of that year's on-field struggle. It was the first Series to be televised, the first to produce total receipts of over $2 million, the first in the twentieth century in which a black man played – Jackie Robinson had joined the Dodgers that year – and the first in which relief pitchers – Hugh Casey for the Dodgers and Joe Page for the Yankees – played a major role for both teams. It was also unusual because many of its most memorable moments were provided by players who were anything but household names. Three of those who immortalized themselves in baseball's book of legends – Floyd Bevens, Al Giofriddo and Cookie Lavagetto – never played another game in the major leagues.

In the fourth game, one of the most dramatic in World Series history, rookie Henry Taylor started for Brooklyn, and Floyd Bevens, with a 7-13 record for the season, started for the Yankees. Taylor walked in a run and lasted only four men, but Bevens, although wild (his ten walks were a Series record), came into the bottom of the ninth pitching a no-hitter. The Yankees had added a second run in the fourth and had threatened without scoring in the ninth (reliever Casey saved the day for Brooklyn); and Brooklyn had scored one run on walks and a sacrifice, bringing the score to 2-1, Yankees, as the Dodgers came to their final at bat.

Bevens got Bruce Edwards to fly out to left,

walked Carl Furillo (Bevens' ninth walk of the game), and got his second out on a fly off Spider Jorgensen. With one out to go, his game was the closest bid for a Series no-hitter to that time. Brooklyn manager Burt Shotton sent Al Gionfriddo in to run for Furillo and put the injured Pete Reiser up to pinch hit for Casey.

Bevens went two-and-one on Reiser. On the next pitch, a ball, Gionfriddo stole second. With the count three-and-one, Yankee manager Bucky Harris, in a controversial call that broke the cardinal rule of never putting the winning run on base, ordered Bevens to walk Reiser.

Brooklyn manager Shotton then sent Cookie Lavagetto up to pinch hit for Eddie Stanky. Although he was a solid player, Lavagetto was past his prime, and had already failed earlier in the Series. But now, in his only hit in seven Series at bats, he caromed Bevens' second pitch off the right field wall, driving in Gionfriddo and Eddie Miksis, who was running for Reiser, to give Brooklyn the winning runs. Lavagetto's double – it was Brooklyn's only hit of the day – cost Bevens the no-hitter and the Yankees the game, 3-2.

5 OCTOBER 1947
Al Gionfriddo's impossible catch

After Cookie Lavagetto's legendary ninth-inning hit stole the fourth game of the 1947 World Series from the Yankees, the Bombers came back to take the fifth game of this dramatic Series from the Dodgers, 2-1. The Dodgers needed the sixth game if they were going to stay in the running, and take it they did, but not before Brooklyn's Al Gionfriddo came through with a spectacular catch that is talked about almost as much now as it was then, and is considered by many observers the greatest catch in World Series play.

Trailing 5-4 in the sixth game after five innings, the Dodgers mounted a rally against relief pitcher Joe Page and added four runs in the top of the sixth inning to take an 8-5 lead. Dodger manager Burt Shotton then sent Gionfriddo into left field as a defensive measure when the Yankees came to bat.

Left-hander Joe Hatten walked Yankee George Stirnweiss but logged two outs before Yogi Berra got on base with a single. Next up was Joe DiMaggio. He swung on Hatten's first pitch and sent it screaming toward the left-field bullpen for what appeared to be a certain home run. Here's how sportscaster Red Barber called it: 'Swung on, and belted. It's a long one, deep to left field. Back goes Gionfriddo. Back . . . back . . . back. It may be out of here. No! Gionfriddo makes a one-handed catch against the bullpen fence. Ohhhhh doctor!'

Far left: Dodger Ed Miksis, running for Pete Reiser, slides home with the winning run on Lavagetto's double in game four of the '47 Series.
Left: Cheering teammates carry Cookie Lavagetto into the locker room at Ebbetts Field.
Above: Sportscaster Red Barber, who gave an exciting account of Gionfriddo's impossible catch.

Above: Al Gionfriddo's one-handed game-saving catch.
Right: Satchel Paige and Bill Veeck as Paige signs his contract with the Cleveland Indians.

Gionfriddo, in what seemed like a futile effort, had taken off after an apparent three-run homer that was destined to tie the score. But outrunning the ball, the left-handed outfielder looked over his right shoulder moments before he reached the 415-foot marker, turned, leaped high into the air, and caught the ball just over the bullpen fence. The crowd exploded. DiMaggio, who had already had time to reach second base, stopped and shook his head in disbelief, then kicked the dirt in frustration. The Yankees managed one more run, but lost the game, 8-6.

The Yankees took the seventh and final game of the Series with Gionfriddo on the bench, his accustomed place. That play was his entire big-league career. 'Branch Rickey told me that if I went to Montreal and had a good year he'd bring me back. I hit .310 with 25 home runs and close to 100 runs batted in, and I didn't come back.' He never appeared in the majors again.

Nowadays at Al's Dugout, Gionfriddo's modest cafe in Goleta, California, customers still ask him if he is *the* Al Gionfriddo. That he is, the one who made the impossible catch. 'Red Barber told me after the game that he witnessed a lot of great catches but mine was an impossible catch.' So it will always be known.

13 AUGUST 1948

Satchel Paige vindicates his legend in the major leagues

Long a legend in the Negro Leagues, LeRoy Robert 'Satchel' Paige was signed by Bill Veeck to the Cleveland Indians on 7 July 1948, becoming the first black pitcher in the American League and the fifth black player in the majors. Jackie Robinson had broken the modern game's color line the year before, and nobody doubted that blacks could play; but Paige, a great showman as well as a great pitcher, and the first player to make good money on the black circuits, was 42 years old in 1948, and few believed he could still have any stuff left on the ball. Many writers accused Veeck of poor taste in his choice of a publicity stunt.

Two days after he joined the Indians, Paige relieved Bob Lemon and pitched two scoreless innings against the Browns; six days later he won his first major-league game with three and a half scoreless innings against the A's.

On 13 August, 51,013 paying spectators, the most ever to see a night game at Comiskey Park, jammed the stadium, and countless others broke through police lines and crowded beneath the stands. Their expectations were rewarded when Paige, in his first full major-league game, shut out the White Sox, 5-0. With masterful control, he allowed only five hits, walked no one, and kept the Sox popping up all night with fastballs, hesitation pitches (since outlawed in major-league play) and 'bat dodgers.'

One week later Paige shut out the White Sox again, 1-0, at a game played in Cleveland before 78,382 spectators (the largest crowd ever to attend a night game). This time he walked one man, but gave up only three hits, struck out five, and permitted no Sox player to advance beyond second base. He finished the season with a 6-1 record that was instrumental in helping the Indians take the American League flag in that year's tight pennant race.

His major-league career had its ups and downs, due largely to health problems, but on 25 September 1965 he pitched three scoreless innings for the Kansas City Athletics, becoming, at 59, the oldest man to appear in a major-league game. He had already been the oldest rookie. Paige became the first man elected to the Hall of Fame by the Committee on Negro Leagues formed in 1971. His prescription for success included: '. . . avoid running at all times, go easy on the vices, and avoid fried foods.' He regretted never having faced Babe Ruth, but not too much, and he made no secret of his feelings about baseball apartheid. His most famous dictum: 'Don't look back . . . something might be gaining on you.'

Top left: Satchel Paige joined the Cleveland Indians midseason in 1948 at the age of 42, and helped pitch the team to a pennant that year.

THE FIFTIES

---
30 SEPTEMBER 1951

Jackie Robinson saves a pennant for the Dodgers

Best-remembered as the first black man in modern baseball, Jackie Robinson succeeded not only because he was able to bear up under withering bigotry, but because he was a superb athlete, one of the most exciting players ever to wear a Dodgers uniform. A fierce competitor, he never hesitated to take risks, especially on the basepaths, where he terrorized opposing pitchers. He was equally solid on the field and at bat, where he displayed the kind of spirit that often found him at his best when it mattered most.

In 1951 he batted .338, his second highest average, and came through for the Dodgers on the last day of the regular season with a performance that kept Brooklyn's pennant hopes alive and demonstrated to the world just what kind of a player he was. Leading the Giants by 13 and a half games on 12 August, the Dodgers had watched in dismay as New York edged closer and closer; on 28 September, two days before the end of the regular season, the Giants pulled abreast when the Dodgers lost to the Phillies. Both clubs won their next two games and remained deadlocked, with both scheduled to play their final games of the season on 30 September 1951. The Giants won their game but things did not look so great for the Dodgers, who were still battling the Phillies when the news arrived of the Giants' 3-2 victory over Boston.

Behind 6-1 at the end of three innings at Shibe Park, the Dodgers were still trailing 6-2 at the top of the fifth. Then Jackie Robinson knocked out a triple, driving in the only baserunner, and later scored himself. One more Brooklyn run and the score stood at 6-5. But the Phillies came back with two runs of their own in the fifth, widening their lead to 8-5.

In the eighth inning the Dodgers added three runs to tie the game. Then Don Newcombe came in to pitch for the Dodgers and Robin Roberts for the Phils, and both pitchers eliminated all batters until the bottom of the twelfth, when Newcombe tired and the Phillies loaded the bases. With two out, Eddie Waitkus socked a low line drive up the middle into the growing gloom – it looked like it was all over for the Dodgers. But Robinson sprinted to his right, flung himself full-length, and caught the ball inches above the ground, all but knocking himself out in the effort.

Above: Jackie Robinson at bat. Robinson kept the Dodgers' pennant hopes alive on 31 September 1951, when he pumped out a triple, made a game-saving catch, and came through with the game-winning home run.
Right: The Dodger pitcher walks dejectedly off the mound as Bobby Thomson is mobbed at home plate after his pennant-winning three-run homer.

It was several minutes before he was able to rise and wobble toward the dugout.

In the fourteenth inning, when it looked like the tie might go on forever, Robinson came to bat with two men out and hammered a Roberts curve into the upper left-field stands, putting the Dodgers one up, 9-8. Bud Podbielan was now pitching (he had replaced Newcombe in the thirteenth), and the Dodgers held the Phillies scoreless for the last of the fourteenth to win one of baseball's most exciting games and keep their pennant hopes alive.

It was a brief reprieve. The Giants downed the Dodgers in an exciting three-game playoff that ended with Bobby Thomson's famous home run. Brooklyn lost the pennant, but Jackie Robinson, despite his team's defeat, finished the 1951 season with an exemplary performance that has grown no less lustrous with the passage of time.

42

3 OCTOBER 1951

Bobby Thomson's 'home run heard 'round the world'

Bobby Thomson will never be remembered with Babe Ruth and Hank Aaron for hitting record numbers of home runs, but as long as baseball exists he will be remembered for hitting one home run in particular. His 'Home Run Heard 'Round the World' not only clinched the 1951 pennant for the Giants, but with the passage of time has come to stand as the eternal symbol of ninth-inning diehard hopes.

In 1951 the Giants got off to a slow start. By 11 August they had managed to creep into second place, but were still a hopeless 13 and a half games behind the league-leading Dodgers. The next day, however, the Giants began a streak that elevated one of baseball's greatest standing rivalries into one of the most exciting pennant races ever. Beginning on 12 August the Giants won 16 games in a row, eventually posting 37 wins out of their final 44 games. With two games left to play in the season they pulled into a tie with the Dodgers. Only a late inning home by Jackie Robinson against the Phils kept the Giants from the flag and forced them into a three-game playoff with the Dodgers.

Thanks to a two-run homer from Bobby Thomson, whose bat had heated up late in the season, the Giants took the first playoff game, 3-1. The Dodgers responded by taking the second game, 10-0. Both teams knew that the winner of the next game – scheduled for 1:30 PM at the Polo Grounds on 3 October 1941 – would face the Yankees in the World Series.

Twenty-game-winner Don Newcombe pitched for the Dodgers on that fateful day, 23-game-winner Sal Maglie for the Giants. Jackie Robinson knocked Pee Wee Reese home with a single in the first inning, and the Dodgers added three more in the eighth, taking a 4-1 lead before the final inning. Then Newcombe began to tire, and Alvin Dark got a single to begin the Giants' ninth; a single from Don Mueller moved Dark to third. Monte Irvin popped out, but a double from Whitey Lockman scored Dark and moved Mueller to third. At this point, with the tying runs on base and only one out, Dodger manager Charlie Dressen retired Newcombe and called in Ralph Branca. Bobby Thomson was next up.

'If you ever hit one,' Giant manager Leo Durocher rasped to Thomson, 'hit one now.' Years later Thomson recalled, 'I could see Leo was as excited as I was and it calmed me down. Going back to the plate I said to myself, You're a pro. Act like one. Do a good job.' Thomson's blundering baserunning had killed the only Giant rally of that game, and he had also made two fielding errors in the Dodgers' three-run eighth inning; he may have felt he had something to make up.

Thomson took Branca's first pitch for a called strike. But the second was so much to his liking that he sent it out of the park, over the head of left fielder Andy Pafko, who stood watching helplessly at the fence. Hardly able to catch his breath for excitement, Thomson rounded the bases and was greeted at home with one of the most sensational welcomes any baseball hero has ever received. Branca wept on the clubhouse steps: the Giants had won the game, 5-4, and the pennant, and a new baseball legend was born.

17 APRIL 1953

Mickey Mantle's 565-foot tape measure homer

By 1953 photographed chewing gum while playing center field and obviously at home, Mickey Mantle was well on his way toward permanent installment in the Ruth-Gehrig-DiMaggio pantheon of Yankee superstars. He had been touted as the most promising player ever when he came up to the Yankees in 1951, the final year of DiMaggio's career (Branch Rickey had offered the Yankees Ralph Kiner and $500,000 for Mantle before he ever played a major-league game), but his rookie performance had been disappointing. In his first full season with the Yankees, however, in 1952, the 20-year-old led the club with a batting average of .311 and was its second-best home run hitter, with 23. The kid was on his way.

Mickey Mantle would play 18 seasons with the Yankees – 12 of them pennant years – and in the process establish himself as 'The Switcher' who could hit left-handed as far as Ruth and right-handed as far as Foxx. Of course he was also the fastest baserunner in the league and had an arm like a cannon. After his first few years, when he had lived down replacing fellow center fielder Joe DiMaggio, he was also the American League's most popular player.

But he was already showing what his incomparable combination of speed and power could do in 1953, and in so doing created a new major-league institution, the 'tape-measure' homer. On 17 April 1953 Mickey Mantle connected with a ball in old Griffith Stadium in Washington, driving it over the

Above: Mickey Mantle crosses the plate after his homer.
Below: The path of Mantle's towering home run.

left-field fence, over the bleachers, and halfway up the scoreboard behind the bleachers where, after just nicking the side of the scoreboard, it flew out of the park and landed across the street. Inspired by the drama of the moment, Yankee press agent Red Patterson found a tape measure and measured the distance of the homer. The next day the papers carried the news that Mantle had hit the ball 565 feet, and the tape-measure homer was born.

The next year Mantle led the league in runs scored, and in 1955 he won his first home run title with 37 round-trippers. In 1956, perhaps his best all-round season and the first of his three MVP years, he belted 52 home runs, and belted in 130 runs with a .353 average. Only three other men have hit 50 homers and batted .350 or better in the same season: Hack Wilson (1930), Jimmie Foxx (1932) and Babe Ruth, who did it three times.

Mantle's 54 home runs in 1961 is still the record for a switch hitter; in 10 different games, he hit home runs batting left-handed and right-handed. He will always be remembered as one of the greatest power hitters, a reputation which is all the more remarkable because he played almost his entire career with injuries and illnesses so severe they would have sidelined a lesser man. As teammate Elston Howard remarked of the man he considered the greatest competitor and the most inspiring leader he had ever known, 'If he had been physically sound for a full season he would have hit 70 homers.'

18 JUNE 1953

The Red Sox score a record 17 runs in one inning

When the Red Sox scored 17 runs against the Detroit Tigers on 17 June 1953 for a final score of 17-1, The Tigers, who had won only 14 of 57 games that year and had clearly taken up residence at the bottom of the league to stay, were at least able to console themselves with the thought that the worst was over. Nightmarish as that game had been, it was not the sort of catastrophe that any team could reasonably expect to suffer with regularity. Little did they know that on the very next day, when they again faced the Red Sox, they would lose by an even greater margin; and that this time, when the Red Sox scored 17 runs, it would happen in one inning.

Ned Garver was starting pitcher for the Tigers on 18 June 1953. He turned in a credible job until the sixth inning, when Boston began hitting him and broke a 3-3 tie. Steve Gromek, a 12-year veteran and recent acquisition of the Tigers who had won as many as 19 games a season for the Indians, was brought in to replace Garver. He managed to retire the side, but not before Boston had upped the score to 5-3, their favor.

It was in the seventh inning that all hell broke loose. Gromek, in his first pitching appearance with the Tigers, lasted for nine runs, all earned, giving up six hits – including a home run by Dick Gernert – and three walks. All together 23 Red Sox batters came to the plate for a total of 11 singles, two doubles, one homer and six bases on balls.

Gromek recalls, 'They got some clean hits, but most of them were flukes. The ball kept bouncing just out of reach of our infielders or falling in front of our outfielders.' After Gromek was lifted by Tiger manager Fred Hutchinson, the Red Sox knocked eight more runs out of replacements Dick Weik and Earl Harrist that inning, for a final score of 23-3. The Red Sox had scored an unprecedented 17 runs in one inning.

Sixteen of the more eccentric major-league records were broken by the Red Sox in their phenomenal inning. Gene Stephens, Sox outfielder, got three hits in the seventh, including a double and two singles; Sammy White and Tom Umphlett also reached base three times. Of the 27 hits the Red Sox logged for the game, Billy Goodman hit five, White got four, and Stephens and Umphlett each got three.

The endless inning lasted 48 minutes. Only 3198 fans witnessed the atrocity, and the Tigers may have felt that if everyone would just keep quiet the event would soon be forgotten. But a humiliation of this magnitude exercises a peculiar fascination over baseball fans, and the day the Red Sox got 17 runs in one inning is likely to be remembered as long as people play with bats and balls.

A newspaper account illustrates the Red Sox' incredible feat with a picture of the scoreboard.

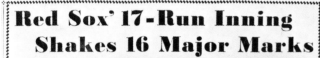

Red Sox' 17-Run Inning Shakes 16 Major Marks

Gene Stephens' Three Safe Hits New Record; Three on Base 3 Times

By HY HURWITZ
BOSTON, Mass.

One of the weakest hitting clubs in recent Red Sox history produced the greatest batting show of modern times when Lou Boudreau's men racked up a 17-run inning while walloping the Tigers, 23 to 3, at Fenway Park, June 18.

Following a 17 to 1 trouncing of Detroit the previous day, the Red Sox, who collected 14 hits and six passes in that inning, established one all-time major league record and tied eight others, set six modern marks and one American League standard in the one nerry-go-round.

One of the most fantastic individual marks—three hits in one inning—by 20-year-old Gene Stephens, who entered the game with a .210 batting average, almost didn't happen. Only for the fact that Manager Lou Boudreau had one spare outfielder left—Hoot Evers, who was nursing a lame back—was Stephens permitted to go to bat a third time in the historic seventh.

Gene had put on an amazing burst of speed in his second time at bat that inning to stretch a routine single into a double. He had hit a normal grounder between first and second and directly at Right Fielder Bob Nieman. He legged it for second and made it, but in the process he hurt something in his neck.

• • •

Gene Ignores Injury

But Gene, stiff neck and all, went to bat for a third time and came through with a sizzling single into right field. No modern player had ever made three hits in the same inning.

Until the Sox sent 23 batters to the plate, only four modern players had gone to bat three times in the same frame since 1900. The first one to do it was Ted Williams of the Red Sox against the Philadelphia

Boston Massacre in Figures

AMERICAN LEAGUE											
P		1	2	3	4	5	6	7	8	9	H
35 DETROIT		0	0	0	2	0	1	0			4
16 BOSTON		0	3	0	0	0	2	17			24
33 ST.LOUIS		0									0
18 NEW YORK		0									5

THE STORY ON THE SCOREBOARD AT FENWAY PARK

Freddy Hatfield of the Tigers being the leading principals in a battle of vicious insults. The Sox were steaming mad at the remarks passed on to Piersall by Batts and Hatfield. Piersall got in the final word when he broke up a 3 to 3 tie in the sixth with a two-run single and singled home two runs in the seventh.

Manager Lou Boudreau removed Piersall from the game when Jim was due to bat for a second time.

Hi-Jinks in Hub

Following are the records set and tied during the game, with the previous record holder shown in parentheses:

All-Time Major League Record Set

Most runs batted in, inning, one club—17—Red Sox (15, Chicago vs. Detroit N. L., September 6, 1883, seventh inning; Brooklyn vs. Cincinnati N. L., May 21, 1952, first inning. Former A. L. record—14—Boston vs. Philadelphia, July 4, 1948, seventh inning.)

All-Time Major League Records Tied

Most batters facing pitcher, inning, one club—23—Red Sox (Chicago vs. Detroit N. L., September 6, 1883, seventh inning; Boston vs. Philadelphia, July 4, 1948, seventh inning.)

Most batters facing pitcher three times, inning, one club—5—Red Sox; Sam White, Gene Stephens, Tom Umphlett, Johnny Lipon and George Kell (Chicago vs. Detroit N. L., September 6, 1883, seventh inning; Edward N. Williamson, Thomas E. Burns, Edward N. Pfeffer, Fred E. Goldsmith and William A. Sunday. Former A. L. record—1—Boston vs. Philadelphia, July 4, 1948, seventh inning.)

Long, Robert L. Lowe and Hugh Duffy, Boston N. L., June 18, 1894, morning game, first inning; Harold H. Reese, Brooklyn, May 21, 1952, first inning. Former A. L. record—2—held

SAMMY WHITE crossing the plate with run No. 17.

31 JULY 1954

Joe Adcock hits four homers and a double for the most total bases in one game

When big Joseph Wilbur Adcock debuted with the Cincinnati Reds in 1950 he had been playing baseball for only five years. Unlike Bob Feller, whose father carved out a baseball diamond for him on his farm, or Mickey Mantle, whose father dressed him in a baseball outfit before he could walk, Adcock didn't receive any of the early baseball conditioning that was so important, for instance, to the development of a slugger like Hank Aaron, whose semipro dad taught him to hit bottlecaps with a broomstick to develop his eye.

But Big Joe's dad had made good use of his six-foot-four, 210-pound son on his Louisiana farm, and Joe was a superb physical specimen when the coach at LSU asked him to try out for the baseball team in the spring of 1945. At the time Adcock owned neither spikes nor glove. He caught on quickly. By the time he joined the Milwaukee Braves in 1953, a year he hit 18 home runs, many considered the outstanding first baseman to be the strongest man in baseball.

Adcock let the world know how strong he was in April of 1953 when he became the first National League player ever to hit a ball into the 483-feet-deep center-field bleachers at the Polo Grounds. No batter had ever dropped a ball there during regular league play until Adcock, hitting against Jim Hearn, knocked a fastball 10 rows up into the center-field stands for a drive estimated at 500 feet. It gave the Braves the winning margin over the Giants, 3-2.

A little over one year later, in a game against the Dodgers, Adcock set a record for power hitting that may never be equalled. In five trips to the plate he hit four home runs and a double for a total of 18 bases, a new major-league record for bases in a single game. 'I was using a borrowed bat,' he said, '. . . I broke my regular bat the night before. So I borrowed one from Charlie White. Boy, I could hardly lift the bat. It was the heaviest on the team. . . .'

Adcock got his four home runs off four different pitchers – Don Newcombe, Erv Palica, Pete Wojey and Johnny Podres. He hit two of his homers and his double on first pitches, and two home runs on second pitches, driving in a total of seven runs. His homer in the fifth inning came with two men on, his shot in the third with one man on. His fourth homer, and third in a row, came in the ninth, putting the finishing touches on a 15-7 Braves victory.

While ten other players have hit four home runs in one game, none ever did it off four different pitchers, and none added a fifth extra-base hit to equal Adcock's record total of 18 bases in a single game. Adcock had also hit a homer in the preceding game, and his five home runs in two consecutive games set yet another record.

Above: Teammates greet Joe Adcock and the umpire looks on after the first of his four homers on 31 July 1954.
Right: Willie Mays' famous circus catch.
Below right: Wertz rounds first as runners are hung up between the bases, awaiting the outcome of Mays' attempt.

29 SEPTEMBER 1954

Willie Mays makes his famous World Series catch

Willie Mays feels that he made so many great plays in the field that he cannot pick one which he considers the greatest. Few if any would argue with his point of view. But be that as it may, as far as the public is concerned, the catch that is remembered most and that is often referred to as the most famous of all time was the one Giant Willie Mays made off Indian Vic Wertz in the opening game of the 1954 World Series.

The score was tied 2-2 in the eighth inning. The Indians had runners on first and second, nobody out. Sal Maglie was pitching for the Giants, but had been getting hit, and southpaw Don Liddle was brought in to pitch to the left-handed Wertz. On Liddle's first pitch Wertz connected, smashing a line drive deep into center field over Mays' head. Willie had begun running on Wertz's swing, and continued running full speed with his back to the plate, arms outstretch-

ed and glove up, until the ball fell into his glove while he was running flat out about ten feet from the fence, 460 feet from home plate. Before he went sprawling he got a throw off to the infield which prevented the runner on second from taking more than one base.

Liddle then retired the next batters. Mays' amazing play had effectively kept the Indians from winning in nine innings and enabled the Giants to win the game, 5-2.

Mays himself claims that a play that gave him more satisfaction occurred that same season at Ebbets Field, when Brooklyn pinch hitter Bobby Morgan sent a ball to left center close to the wall. Running as fast as he could, at the last instant he threw himself headfirst with his glove outstretched and was knocked unconscious when he hit the wall. The umpire rolled him over and took the ball out of his glove; when Willie came to, he had to ask manager Leo Durocher if he had made the catch.

Mays also feels that he made a much more difficult play also off Wertz, in the tenth inning of the same '54 World Series game in which he had made his famous eighth-inning catch. Although it seemed that

47

hardly anybody appreciated the skill involved, on that occasion, with the score tied, Wertz slammed a screwball 440 feet up the left-center slot. It bounced viciously between the outfielders and appeared headed for an inside-the-park home run but Mays, again running at top speed, managed to grab it back-handed, and limited Wertz to a double.

And what gave Mays his greatest kick as a major-league player? Although no one, including Mr. Mays, would ever question his fielding ability, Willie Mays remembers with greatest satisfaction the time on 30 April 1961 when he pulled out of a deep batting slump and hit four home runs, driving in eight, in a single game against the Braves. Only four other men have hit four homers in a nine-inning game since the turn of the century, but no one has done it since.

4 OCTOBER 1955

Sandy Amoros' catch saves the Series for the Dodgers

In the 10-year span between 1947 and 1956 there were six World Series between the Brooklyn Dodgers and the New York Yankees, and each one was special. The Dodgers – 'The Bums' – represented everyman; the Yankees, perennial winners in their league, were the aristocrats. Plebian Brooklyn battled patrician New York.

For a decade the Dodgers had been nearly as dominant in the National League as the Yankees had been in the American, but so far the world championship had eluded them, and the hated Yankees had defeated them in five straight Series contests. 'Wait till next year!' was the Brooklyn battle cry.

In 1955, following a dreadful first season under manager Walter Alston, the Dodgers breezed to the top of their league, 13 and a half games ahead of second-place Milwaukee; and the Yankees, with only a little more difficulty, gave manager Casey Stengel his sixth pennant in seven years. The epic era of subway Series would continue.

The Bums dropped the first two games, sending bar receipts up across Brooklyn. No team had ever bounced back after losing the first two to win in a seven-game Series, and the Dodgers were not known for success in Series play. But then, on his twenty-third birthday, Dodger pitcher Johnny Podres beat the Yankees, 8-3. The Dodgers repeated in the fourth game, taking the Bombers 8-5; and rookie Roger Craig nailed the Yanks again in the fifth game, 5-3, putting the Dodgers ahead three games to two. When Whitey Ford returned the favor to take the sixth game for the

Left: Yogi Berra belts a line drive into left field.
Top three: Sequence photographs depict Sandy Amoros' Series-saving catch and throw.

Yankees, 5-1, the stage was set for the most exciting Dodger-Yankee passion play baseball had ever seen.

Johnny Podres faced Tommy Byrne in game seven. Both had won one game so far in the Series. Seventy thousand fans gathered at Yankee Stadium, and many more watched on that new contraption, television, as Podres, supremely confident, held the Yankees scoreless while the Dodgers scored one run in the fourth inning and another run in the sixth. But in the sixth inning Podres got into a serious jam.

Alston had used a pinch hitter for Don Zimmer in the sixth inning, and now moved to beef up his defense by pulling in Jim Gilliam from left field to replace Zimmer at second. Sandy Amoros, a relatively colorless player who had already pulled a surprise two-run homer in the fifth game of the Series, was sent in to replace Gilliam in left. This is how the Dodger defense stood when Podres walked Billy Martin, and Gil McDougald bunted safely in the sixth, putting the tying runs on base with no men out. Next up in the Yankee batting order were Yogi Berra, Hank Bauer and Moose Skowron.

The Dodger outfield swung to the right for pull-hitter Berra, but Yogi hit a long high fly down the left field line; Martin and McDougald started running. So did Amoros. Racing at least 100 feet to reach the ball, he struck out his glove at the last possible moment, caught the ball, and fired it to Pee Wee Reese, who caught McDougald off base for the double play. Taking heart once more, Podres got Bauer to ground out, ending the inning.

Podres gave up only one more hit in the remaining three innings to win the game, 2-0, handing the Dodgers their first Series victory ever. Amoros, with his much-celebrated, much-photographed catch, had saved the day. But as fate would have it, Brooklyn's first World Series victory was also its last, for the Dodgers did not win another Series until they had moved to a new town – Los Angeles.

Don Larsen's perfect World Series game

By July of 1960 Donald James Larsen, who never won more than 11 games in 14 major-league seasons, was back in the minors; but at Yankee Stadium on 8 October 1956, in the fifth game of the World Series, the 27-year-old right-hander pitched with such excellence that he became a legend in his own time. The rest of his career forgotten, he is still a household name: the only man ever to pitch a perfect game in World Series history.

Larsen began his perfect game by fanning Jim Gilliam, then threw three balls to Pee Wee Reese before striking him out. It was the only time that day that Larsen – who displayed impeccable control changing speeds, and using an unusual no-windup delivery that he had unveiled late in the season – even went over two balls on a batter.

After Reese, he got Duke Snider to line out to Hank Bauer in right. Snider was the first of 27 consecutive batters Larsen cut down that day (Gilliam and Reese were two of his seven strikeouts). It took Larsen 15 pitches to retire the side in the first inning, and thereafter he never threw more than 15 pitches an inning.

Strong fielding from his Yankee teammates saved Larsen's perfect game five times. A sharp liner off Jackie Robinson's bat jumped out of third baseman Andy Carey's glove in the second inning, but was fielded in time by shortstop Gil McDougald. In the fifth inning, Mickey Mantle, racing to deep left center, made a dramatic back-handed catch of a liner by Gil Hodges. Mantle also hit a homer off Sal Maglie – one of only five hits the Dodger pitcher gave up – for New York's first run. The other run of the game came two innings later, in the sixth, on a single by Carey, a sacrifice by Larsen, and a single by Bauer.

Sandy Amoros almost ruined Larsen's game in the fifth when he hit a liner that turned foul just before slamming into the seats for what would have been a

home run. In the seventh, McDougald saved the day with a nice pickup of a short-hop smash off Gilliam; and in the eighth, Carey caught a dangerous low liner off Hodges that came at him inches off the ground to the left of third base.

By the eighth inning, every pitch brought a gasp from the crowd. When Larsen came to bat in the bottom of the eighth, the 65,000 fans at Yankee Stadium rose to their feet to give him the ovation of his life. Only six men since 1876 had ever pitched perfect games; no one had ever done it in a Series.

Until then Larsen had been the picture of non-chalance but, in his own words, 'I was so weak in the knees out there in the ninth inning I thought I was going to faint. My legs were rubbery, and my fingers didn't feel like they were on my hand. I said to myself, "Please help me out, somebody."'

With three outs to go, Larsen got Carl Furillo to fly out. He got Roy Campanella to bounce out, but not before Campy hit a long drive that went foul just before it would have become a home run. Slugger Dale Mitchell was sent in to bat for Sal Maglie; it was at this point that Larsen turned his back on the batter and muttered his prayer for help.

Larsen's first pitch went wide, a ball; on the second, Mitchell swung and missed; the third he fouled into the stands. The fans were on the edges of their seats. Larsen's next throw shaved the outside corner, umpire Babe Pinelli called it a strike, and all hell broke loose. The Yankees had won, 2-0, and Larsen had carved a place for himself in baseball eternity.

50

26 MAY 1959

Harvey Haddix pitches a perfect game – and loses!

On the cold, dank night of 26 May 1959, 35-year-old left-hander Harvey Haddix opened for the Pirates against the Braves at Milwaukee's County Stadium. Haddix, who had won 20 games as a rookie with the Cardinals in 1953, had been only an average starter since, and was not having a good year. At present he was fighting off a cold and a bad cough. He got into bed when his team arrived at Milwaukee that afternoon, and would have stayed there if he hadn't been slated to pitch.

In the first inning the diminutive Haddix got Johnny O'Brien to ground to short, Eddie Mathews to line out to Rocky Nelson, and Henry Aaron to fly out to Bill Virdon. Using the fastball and slider he was to employ most of that night, he continued the next inning by striking out Joe Adcock, and got Wes Covington and Del Crandall to hit easy groundouts. His own team failed to score, but Haddix himself got a single and advanced to third before the end of the inning.

In the third, fourth and fifth innings Haddix retired the Braves in order. He was by now aware that he was working on a no-hitter but, thinking he had walked someone along the way, had no idea that he was also working on a perfect game.

An unpleasant drizzle began as Haddix headed to the mound in the bottom of the seventh. The Pirates were still scoreless; Lew Burdette, pitching for the Braves, gave up occasional hits, but retired all the Pirates he faced in the sixth, seventh and eighth innings. Haddix got O'Brien and Aaron on bouncers to third and struck out Mathews in the seventh. He struck out Adcock and got Covington and Crandall to hit into outs in the eighth.

The Buc's Bill Virdon got as far as third base in the top of the ninth, but did not score. In the bottom, Haddix struck out Andy Pafko, got Johnny Logan to fly out to Bob Skinner, and finally faced opposing pitcher Lew Burdette, who yelled to Haddix, 'I'll break up your no-hitter.' Haddix struck him out. He had pitched a perfect game – only seven other perfect games had been pitched since 1876 – but the game was not over.

When he retired O'Brien in the tenth inning, Haddix became the first pitcher ever to retire 28 men in a row. In the tenth, eleventh and twelfth innings he

Top left: Don Larsen delivers the third strike for the final out in the ninth inning to clinch the first – and only – perfect game hurled in Series history.
Below left: Catcher Yogi Berra and Don Larsen embrace after Larsen's landmark achievement.
Top right: Harvey Haddix winds up for a pitch.
Above right: Haddix enters the dugout after pitching 12 innings of perfect baseball – and losing.

made history again: by keeping the Braves hitless and scoreless, he became the first man to pitch a perfect game for more than nine innings, as well as the first to pitch a no-hitter for more than 11 innings. But his team had still not scored.

They were still scoreless when Burdette gave up his twelfth hit in the top of the thirteenth. Pirate manager Danny Murtaugh suggested to Haddix that he might be content with having pitched the greatest game in history, but the pitcher refused to pass on his chance for a win. In the thirteenth, Felix Mantilla became the first of 37 batters Haddix faced that day to get on base (it took a throw from third that was ruled an error). Mathews bunted Mantilla to second, and Aaron was purposely walked. Then Joe Adcock met Haddix's second pitch – 'my only bad pitch' – and dropped it over the fence, driving in the winning runs. So it was that Harvey Haddix lost the best-pitched game ever recorded in the history of baseball.

THE SIXTIES

13 OCTOBER 1960

Bill Mazeroski hits the most timely home run in World Series history

The last time previous to 1960 the Pirates had faced the Yankees in World Series play, in 1927, the Window Breakers retired the Pittsburgh Nine in four straight games. This time, a Pittsburgh team with its first pennant since 1927 faced another awesome Yankee team, one that had just come from 15 straight victories and represented manager Casey Stengel's tenth flag in 12 seasons.

This is not to say that the Pirates weren't a solid team, defensively and offensively. Second baseman Bill Mazeroski, that year's leader in National League fielding, handled the double-play pivot and throw from his position better than any player in history; Pittsburgh's shortstop Dick Groat, leading the league in batting with .325, was seconded by the Pirates' great outfielder Roberto Clemente, with .314. But the Yankees, with Mantle and Maris, came from a tradition of excellence, and in this Series they would set Series records for club batting average (.338 against the Buc's .256), runs (55 to the Buc's 27), hits (91 to Pittsburgh's 60), and home runs (10 to the Pirates' 4); and register the most decisive shutout in Series history (12-0 in the sixth game). History remembers best, however, that in this most unpredictable of all Series the Pirates won the seventh and deciding game.

Left: An exuberant mob greets Bill Mazeroski at home plate after his Series-winning home run.
Above: Bill Mazeroski and Dick Groat (right) embrace in the locker room after the Pirates' victory.
Right: Warren Spahn delivering a pitch.

On that day Vernon 'Deacon' Law, looking for his third Series win, started for the Pirates; Bullet Bob Turley started for the Yanks. By the end of the second inning the Pirates, playing to the home crowd at Forbes Field, had pulled out in front, 4-0. But the Yanks scored in the fifth, and added four more in the sixth, taking the lead, 5-4. Two more New York runs in the top of the eighth left the Bucs facing a 7-4 Yankee lead.

A break came the Pirates' way when a grounder off the bat of their Bill Virdon, which looked like it was headed into a double play, took a bad hop and hit second baseman Tony Kubek instead. Thereupon a single from Dick Groat scored Gino Cimoli, the Pirates got tying runs in scoring position, and Clemente beat out an infield hit to score Virdon, leaving the Pirates only one run behind. Seconds later Hal Smith delivered a home run that brought three runs in, putting the Buc's in front 9-7 and turning Forbes Field into a madhouse.

But the Yanks came back in the seventh. Bobby Richardson got on and Mantle drove him in. Then Yogi Berra hit a hopping smash that Rocky Nelson managed to back-hand just beyond first base, the force of the drive spinning him around. While he stepped on first to put Berra out and just missed Mantle diving back for safety, Gil McDougald raced home from third with the tying run. The score was now 9-9.

Enter Bill Mazeroski, whose homer had provided the margin in the first game. First up for the Pirates in the bottom of the ninth, he let Ralph Terry's first pitch go by, then nailed the second some 400 feet over the left center wall to win the game and the Series. Pittsburgh erupted in joyous pandemonium. Mazeroski was a hero. The day was theirs, and Pittsburgh had won its first World Series in 35 years.

28 APRIL 1961

Warren Spahn pitches a no-hitter at the age of 40

Warren Spahn's 363 career wins, a total which many nine-man pitching staffs, added together, will not approach, places him fourth in win totals this century in the august company of Christy Mathewson, Walter Johnson and Grover Cleveland Alexander. Among other records, Spahn leads the major leagues in total wins for a left-hander, and shares with Mathewson the modern record of winning 20 or more games in 13 seasons.

Spahn was a model of longevity and endurance, evoking memories of the early days when pitchers often pitched in 400 or more innings a season. Although not quite that old, he pitched in one of the great eras of baseball against the likes of Musial, Mays, Snider and Koufax, and led the National League in complete games nine times, including seven consecutive years from 1957 through 1963, his last season. His two best seasons, both 23-7 records, were recorded 11 years apart, in 1953 and in 1963 – when Spahn was 42 years old.

Even more remarkable, Spahn did not win his first major-league game until he was 25. Although he came up to the Boston Braves in 1942, he was sent back to the minors by manager Casey Stengel when he refused Stengel's order for a brush-back pitch against Pee Wee Reese. Stengel doubted Spahn's courage, but after three years in the service, during which he won a Purple Heart and a citation for bravery, few did. Beginning in 1947, his first full year with the Braves, Spahn started between 32 and 37 games every year for 17 years; during those 17 years, he never had two consecutive seasons in which he did not win 20 games. When his fastball slowed down in mid-career, he simply became a smarter pitcher. He never stopped learning new pitches, and rarely gave a batter anything good to hit.

Spahn's two no-hitters came late in his career. His first, his twentieth win of the season, came in September of 1960 against the Phillies. The 4-0 victory fell short of a perfect game by two walks. His fastball, humming as good as it ever had, combined with his curves to strike out 15 batters.

His second no-hitter, on 28 April 1961, his third start of his seventeenth season, was even better, even though he had no working margin and the Giant team he faced was far stronger than the Phillies club he had no-hit the year before. But according to Spahn, 'It was so easy it was pathetic. Everything went my way and they kept guessing wrong. But let's face it: I was just plain lucky.'

Once again he walked two men – each time at the start of an inning – '. . . a cardinal sin with a one-run lead.' But only twice in the first eight innings was the no-hitter in doubt. In the sixth, shortstop Roy McMillan fumbled a Jose Pagan grounder before throwing him out; and in the seventh, McMillan had trouble with a Harvey Kuenn grounder, but again recovered in time to throw him out. The real excitement came in the crucial ninth inning.

Spahn had two strikes on lead-off batter Ed Bailey when Bailey hit a pop foul. Catcher Charlie Lau dropped it. Then Bailey fouled off the next four pitches, giving Spahn his worst moment of the game – 'He was swinging good' – until the wiley left-hander finally managed to slip a third strike past him.

Next up Matty Lou laid a bunt down the first base line which Spahn fielded and threw to Joe Adcock for the out. Only one out remained. Spahn faced pinch hitter Joey Amalfitano, who smashed a hard grounder to shortstop McMillan. For the third time that day McMillan had trouble hanging on to it, but once again he got the ball off to Adcock in time for the out, and Warren Spahn had his second no-hitter, 1-0. Coming five days after his fortieth birthday, it made him just a bit younger than Cy Young was when he became the oldest man ever to score a no-hitter, his third, on 20 June 1908, at the age of 41.

Above right: A young Spahn warms up with his classic, high-kick wind-up.
Right: Maris beats out a grounder on 21 May 1961.

1 OCTOBER 1961

Roger Maris sets a new home run record

'Every day and every night people wanted to talk to me. . . . People who knew nothing about baseball were there in the clubhouse – and they all asked the same damn question: "Do you think you can break Babe Ruth's record?"'

'How the hell should I know?' was the reply that public and press, likely as not, received from Roger Maris that season.

A great slugger, but unlike The Bambino a man who did not enjoy his public and was sometimes moody or even surly, Maris had known by 1 July, along with the rest of the world, that he was within reach of Ruth's 1927 season record of 60 home runs.

On 4 July, Maris slammed his thirty-first home run. He was now more than halfway there. But Roger Maris was an unpopular player caught in the process of committing the unforgivable crime of breaking the most coveted record of the most popular ballplayer in history. Many fans, especially older people, did not want to see Ruth's record broken; others complained that he was going for the record in a 162-game schedule, whereas Ruth had hit his 60 in a 154-game schedule. Incredibly, some Yankee executives even pressured manager Ralph Houk to change the lineup to lessen Maris's chances. If any Yankee was going to break the record, the feeling ran, it ought to be popular Mickey Mantle, who in fact hit a respectable 54 homers that year.

None of this was lost on Maris, who was already laboring under the terrific physical and psychological pressure of going for Babe Ruth's record. About the time Maris hit his fifty-first home run, on 26 August, Commissioner Ford Frick announced that if he broke Ruth's record his feat would go into the record books with an asterisk to indicate that he had done it in a longer season than Ruth. Maris commented, with comparative reserve, 'Do you know any other record that's been broken since they started playing 162 games that's got an asterisk?'

Nevertheless, in the third inning of game 154, fac-ing right-hander Milt Pappas under the precedent-setting glare of the national media, Maris hit home run 59 of the season. In three more at bats that game, the best Maris was able to do was slash a foul that missed being a home run by about ten feet. Quoth Maris: 'I'm glad it's over. The pressure is off.'

But eight more games remained to be played. On 26 September in the third inning of a game against the Orioles, Maris drove a pitch from Jack Fisher into the sixth row of the third deck of Yankee Stadium for his sixtieth home run of the season, becoming the only man to equal Ruth's mark. Thoroughly unhappy with media and fans alike, Maris was finally persuaded by his teammates to emerge from the dugout to acknow-ledge the ovation from a hometown crowd which included Babe Ruth's widow, Claire.

Maris took the next day off, claiming he needed a rest. Then, three games later, on the last day of the season, he connected with a pitch from Boston rookie right-hander Tracy Stallard and put it into the stands for home run number 61. For once his stony face relaxed, and he shook hands as he rounded the bases. His teammates formed a human wall in front of the dugout and four times refused him sanctuary until he waved his cap at the cheering crowd. Maris had broken the record, and he had won the game for the Yankees, 1-0.

Top left: Roger Maris clouts his record-breaking sixty-first homer of the season on 1 October 1961.
Left: Maris waves to acknowledge the crowd's roar after hitting home run 61, at Yankee Stadium.
Top: Bobby Richardson throws to first in the third game of the 1962 Series, as Orlando Cepeda slides.
Above: Richardson practices fielding second base.

16 OCTOBER 1962

Bobby Richardson snares Willie McCovey's line drive to clinch the Series for the Yankees

Coming from behind to snatch the 1962 National League pennant from the Dodgers, the San Francisco Giants found themselves facing the New York Yankees, who were looking for their second consecutive Series win. One day of postponement due to rain in New York and three in San Francisco, plus coast-to-coast traveling, made this Series last 13 calendar days, the longest since the Giants and the A's clashed in rain-soaked 1911. In a classic Series dominated by pitching, the Yankees, hitting .199 as a club, registered their lowest batting average in 27 Series appearances. The Giants, hitting a more respectable .226 as a team and outscoring the Yanks 21-20, struggled valiantly, but lost in the dramatic seven-game Series that went right down to the last pitch.

No one was surprised when the top-rated Yankees, with Whitey Ford outpitching the Giants' Billy O'Dell, took the first game, 6-2 (although the Giants ended Ford's record-breaking 33 and two-thirds consecutive scoreless Series innings in the second inning). But the Giants bounced back behind 24-game winner Jack Sanford to take the second game from New York's Ralph Terry with a businesslike 2-0, including a home run by Willie McCovey.

The Yankees returned the favor in the next outing, but the Giants again evened the Series up in the fourth game, thanks largely to a grand slam homer by Chuck Hiller, the first grand slammer ever hit by a National League player in Series competition. A three-run homer by Tom Tresh in the eighth inning gave the Yankees the fifth game, 5-3; but five days later in San Francisco Giant pitcher Billy Pierce threw a three-hitter against the Yanks, and the Giants evened the Series for the third time, 5-2.

In the seventh and final game Ralph Terry faced Jack Sanford for the third time. Each had won one game so far this Series, and in this game each kept his opponents scoreless for the first four innings. The Yankees loaded the bases in the fifth inning and scored one run; they loaded the bases again in the eighth, but O'Neil relieved Sanford and kept them scoreless.

The Giants came to bat in the bottom of the ninth trailing by one run. Matty Alou beat out a bunt and got on first, but Ralph Terry struck out the next two batters. Then Willie Mays came through for a double. Brilliant fielding by Roger Maris kept Alou from scoring, but still left the Giants with the tying and winning runs on second and third base.

Next up was powerful Willie McCovey, who had already homered off Terry this Series. Terry, who could not help remembering how Bill Mazeroski had homered off him to snatch victory from the Yankees in the last inning of the 1960 Series, conferred with manager Ralph Houk, and bravely decided to pitch to him. 'A man seldom gets the kind of second chance I did,' he said later. McCovey was in fact a much more dangerous hitter than Mazeroski ever had been.

On the first pitch, McCovey smashed a long foul ball. He took a ball on the second, then shot a smoking drive toward right field. Bobby Richardson, at second base, who barely had time to throw up his glove, made a catch that surprised even himself. The game was over, 1-0; the Yankees had won the Series.

Left: Stan Musial is congratulated in the dugout after making hit 3431 on 19 May 1962.
Top: 'Stan the Man' Musial cranks a long ball in spring training.
Above: Pete Rose is joined by Stan Musial to celebrate his breaking of Musial's National League hitting record on 10 August 1981.

29 SEPTEMBER 1963

Stan Musial collects his 3630th hit in his final at bat

On 17 September 1941 Stanley Frank Musial played his first game as a Cardinal. He got two hits, and his team won the game, 3-2. Twenty-two years later, still a Cardinal and one of the great names in baseball, he played his last game. He got two hits, and his team won the game, 3-2.

It was not until mid-August that the 42-year-old veteran finally made up his mind that 1963 would be his last season. The year before Stan the Man had appeared in 135 games, hit 19 home runs, 82 RBI's, and averaged .325 against right-handers and .345 against left-handers. He was still having fun. But in 1963 he found that he wasn't able to concentrate at bat as completely as he had previously, so he decided to call it quits.

Musial began his twenty-second year of play with a hit, and on 8 May 1963, playing against the Dodgers, he broke Babe Ruth's career record for extra-base hits when he blasted a home run off Bob Miller. In his last All-Star appearance, on 9 July, he lined out to Al Kaline in right field, but on 11 September, after he had already decided to call it quits, he celebrated the birth of a grandson the previous day by slamming a two-run round-tripper off Glen Hobbie of the Cubs.

His Cardinals were on a streak, taking 19 of 20 to move within one game of the league-leading Dodgers, who came to St Louis for a crucial series late in September. Although the Dodgers won the game and swept the series, in the seventh inning of the first contest Musial hit career home run number 475, causing great commotion among St Louis fans.

By now photographers and reporters were following him everywhere: a great baseball career was coming to an end. On 29 September 1963, the Cardinals' last game of the season and Stan Musial's last game ever, the day dawned gray and cold. While Musial was suiting up he joked with a reporter, who informed him that he had 3628 hits, and casually remarked that he would like to make it 3630, for the sake of round numbers, but that it wouldn't worry him if he didn't get any hits. Pre-game ceremonies attended by all of baseball's high officialdom lasted about an hour. Musial remarked, 'As long as I live, I'll always remember this game.'

He struck out in the first inning, but in the fourth he slashed a one-one pitch past the Reds' pitcher Jim Maloney into center field for hit number 3629. In the sixth inning, in his third at bat in a still scoreless game, Musial banged a curve ball past first base into right field, driving in the Cards' first run. It was career hit number 3630 and RBI number 1950 for Stan the Man. At that he was replaced on base by runner Gary Kalb; cheers greeted him as he left the field for the last time. Undoubtedly following the action with some interest was young Cincinnati rookie Pete Rose, who was destined to set some records of his own.

Sandy Koufax pitches a perfect game

From 1961 through 1966, after which an arthritic left elbow forced him into early retirement at the age of 30, Sandy Koufax mowed down batters so mercilessly that some insisted they should be given four strikes when they faced him. Over his career the soft-spoken left-hander averaged better than one strikeout per inning, a feat never approached by any other pitcher. In his last five years his win-loss total was 111-34. Sandy Koufax set more records than we have space to list.

In 1963, when Koufax was 25-5, Yogi Berra remarked, 'I can see how he won 25 games. What I don't understand is how he lost five.' The year 1963 also saw Koufax throw his second no-hitter in as many years. He would throw one in each of the next two seasons, becoming the first major-leaguer to pitch four no-hitters (Nolan Ryan has since throw five, and

Top: Pitching ace Sandy Koufax in the midst of his perfect game over the Cubs on 10 September 1965.
Left: Opposing Cub pitcher Bob Hendley.
Right: Don Drysdale pitching for win 200 with a two-hit performance against the Giants on 26 June 1968.

has also bettered Koufax's 1965 major-league season record of 382 stikeouts by one).

In his first no-hitter, Koufax struck out three batters in nine pitches in the first inning. He fanned 13 altogether, but walked five and went three-and-two on eight other batters. Koufax retired 22 men in a row in his second no-hitter, walking only one, but also registered only four strikeouts. In his third no-hitter, 'I had tremendous stuff,' he recalls. Only one man – his only walk – reached base, and Koufax faced only 27 batters, striking out 12.

Koufax was 21-7 going into his fourth no-hitter, his perfect game on 9 September 1965. But he had lost his last five starts, and he had no idea that he would be leading his Dodgers, who had been hitting poorly behind him and were half a game out in a tight pennant race, to a flawless victory over the Cubs. Chicago's lineup featured such slugging threats as Billy Williams, with 34 homers and 108 RBI's that year; Ron Santo, with 33 homers and 101 RBI's; and Ernie Banks, with 28 homers and 108 RBI's.

Koufax got through the early innings on his curve, '. . . the best I had all year,' and then '. . . my fastball really came alive, as good a fastball as I'd had all year.' Almost forgotten is the great performance of Chicago's hurler Bob Hendley, who didn't allow a run until the fifth inning, and that came on a defensive lapse following a walk, a sacrifice, and a successful steal. Dodger Lou Johnson's bloop double in the seventh didn't figure in the 1-0 shutout: this was the only game in major-league history with just one hit.

The Dodgers' one-run lead didn't permit Koufax to relax. His perfect game was jeopardized three times. In the very first inning, a solid fly off Glenn Beckert's bat landed just foul in left field; in the second inning, Willie Davis stopped a hard liner from Byron 'Pidge' Browne from going for extra bases. In the seventh, with two outs, Koufax threw three straight balls to Billy Williams before adding two strikes and getting him to fly out. Had Williams got on, Ron Santo would have been next up.

But with his fastball humming in high gear, Koufax fanned lead-off Santo in the eighth, and then stuck out Banks and Browne. In the ninth he struck out Chris Krug and Joey Amalfitano, and then faced his final batter, Harvey Kuenn, a .303 lifetime hitter who had so far struck out only 15 times in 1965.

Going at Kuenn, power against power, Koufax struck him out with three fastballs, ending the landmark game with six straight strikeouts. He had fanned seven of the last nine men he faced for a total of 14 strikeouts, a good index of just how much stuff he had on the ball that day.

Koufax had only one more painful season left – he set a new National League left-handers' season record of 27 wins in 1966 and again took the Dodgers to the Series – before arthritis forced his early retirement. It was performances such as his perfect game that got him elected into the Hall of Fame despite his injury-shortened career total of only 165 wins.

Don Drysdale sets the all-time record of 58 and two-thirds consecutive scoreless innings

For much of Donald Scott Drysdale's 13 full seasons with the Dodgers he played in the shadow of the great Sandy Koufax, much as Lou Gehrig played in the shadow of Babe Ruth during his heyday. But before he retired, Drysdale recorded more victories, more shutouts, pitched more innings, and struck out more batters than any other Dodger in history.

Honored with a Cy Young Award for his 25-9 performance in 1962, he three times led the National League in strikeouts (fanning more than 200 batters six times); four times recorded more than 300 innings; 12 consecutive times pitched more than 200 innings; and played on five pennant-winning and three world championship teams. But of all his impressive achievements, Drysdale made his most indelible mark in 1968, in the twilight of his career, when he threw six consecutive shutouts and set a new all-time major-league record of 58 and two-thirds consecutive scoreless innings.

On 14 May 1968 Don Drysdale shut out the Cubs, 1-0, yielding two hits. Four days later, yielding five hits, he stopped Houston, 1-0. On 22 May, in a classic duel with the Cardinals' Bob Gibson, he allowed five hits to Gibson's three, but won the game, 2-0. Four days later he gave up six hits, but shut out the Houston Astros, 5-0.

On 31 May Drysdale threw a 3-0, six-hit shutout against the Giants before 50,000 fans at Dodger Stadium. With his string of scoreless innings standing at 44, the Giants made him sweat for his forty-fifth when Willie McCovey led off the Giant ninth with a walk. A single by Jim Ray Hart and a walk to Jim Marshall loaded the bases, no men out.

The count on Dick Dietz went to two-and-two when an inside pitch clipped Dietz on the left arm. But – to the Giants' dismay – the umpire ruled that Dietz had not made a reasonable effort to get out of the way. When play was resumed Drysdale got Dietz to fly out, and retired the side. Dodger Stadium exploded in celebration of his fifth consecutive shutout.

On 4 June Drysdale got his sixth straight shutout – setting a new all-time major-league record – when he zapped the Pittsburgh Pirates, 5-0, allowing only three hits. He had tied the major-league consecutive shutout record set by Guy 'Doc' Harris in 1904 with his fifth straight shutout; his 4 June victory also broke the National League record of 46 and a third consecutive scoreless innings set by Carl Hubbell in 1933. Only one record remained to be shattered, Walter Johnson's 56 consecutive scoreless innings, set in 1913, 55 years before.

On 8 June Drysdale took the mound against the Phillies. He kept them scoreless for the first two innings, breaking Johnson's all-time record when he retired Roberto Pena on a ground ball to open the third inning. Not until the fifth inning did the streak finally come to an end. Two singles followed by a pop fly from Howie Bedell enabled the first run against Drysdale to score in almost a month, and froze his scoreless inning streak at 58 and two-thirds.

Ironically, except for this incredible streak, 1968 was not a great year for Drysdale. He finished the season with 14-12 record and, following a 5-4 record in 1969, retired from baseball. Retired, but not forgotten: few screenwriters could have scripted a more appropriate ending to a distinguished pitching career than Don Drysdale's 58 and two-thirds inning record, a streak no one has approached since 1913.

Denny McLain wins his thirtieth game of the season

During the few years that 'Mighty Mouth' Dennis Dale McLain sparkled on the mound, he dazzled batters with a superb assortment of fastballs, overhand curves and baffling sliders, all delivered with precise control. In 1968 at the age of 24, the outspoken right-hander led his Tigers to the pennant with 31 wins and six losses, becoming the first major-league pitcher to win 30 games since Dizzy Dean 34 years before him, and the first American Leaguer since Lefty Grove 37 years before.

Unlike Grove and Dean, who got four of their wins in relief, McLain came by all of his as a starter, taking the league MVP and the first of two consecutive Cy Young Awards in 1968 with the league-leading statistics of 31 wins in 41 starts, 28 complete games, and 336 innings pitched (and with 241 hits, 280 strikeouts, six shutouts and an ERA of 1.96).

In 1965, his second full year with the Tigers, McLain was 16-6. The next year he won 20 games, but when he dropped to a 17-16 record in 1967, the Tigers

tried unsuccessfully to trade their reckless extrovert. They failed.

McLain began the 1968 season by dropping his first two starts, but then, pitching every fourth game, he won 23 of his first 26 decisions. By 3 July, with the season less than half over, he logged his fifteenth win, and sportswriters began tracking his progress as they had followed Roger Maris in 1961. On 27 July McLain won his twentieth game, making him the first pitcher to win 20 in July since Lefty Grove. On the last day of the month he won his twenty-first.

On 14 September 1968, facing the Oakland Athletics, McLain was looking for his thirtieth win. Dizzy Dean had come 1400 miles to witness the event, but it was not one of McLain's great games. Reggie Jackson homered twice off him, and the A's were ahead 4-3 going into the bottom of the ninth. Any other pitcher would probably have been pulled by then.

Pinch hitting for McLain, Al Kaline walked to lead off the bottom of the Tigers' ninth. Dick McAuliffe fouled out, but a Mickey Stanley single to center put Kaline on third. Jim Northrup hit a weak grounder which first baseman Danny Cater scooped up and fired to stop Kaline at the plate, but his throw was wide and Kaline scored, Stanley moving to third on the error. With the score tied at 4-4, Willie Horton lined a drive over the head of left fielder Jim Gosger, Stanley scored, and McLain had his thirtieth win. He notched number 31 his next time out.

Throwing 24-9 in the next year, McLain became the first repeat Cy Young Award winner in American League history (sharing it with Mike Cuellar). In 1970, however, his career took a deadly tailspin when he was suspended by commissioner Bowie Kuhn for gambling on games. Returning to action on 1 July, overweight and out of shape, McLain was way off form. He was suspended again on 9 September for carrying a gun and finished the 1970 season with a 3-5 record. Unloaded to the Senators for 1971, he again led the league, but this time in losses, with 22.

After one more year, split between Oakland and the Atlanta Braves, going 4-7, McLain was out of baseball at 28 years of age. Thereafter his fall was meteoric. Right now Dennis Dale McLain is behind bars facing up to 75 years in prison for convictions on loan-sharking, bookmaking, extortion and possession of cocaine. But despite the tragic ending, his 31 wins in 1968 stand as a remarkable display of pitching excellence, and have not been seriously challenged since.

Top left: Don Drysdale blows a fastball past the batter.
Far left: Danny McLain pitches to Rick Monday in the first inning of the game in which the right-hander clinched his thirtieth win.
Left: Al Kaline hugs McLain after the Tigers scored the winning run against the Oakland A's on 14 September 1968, to give McLain his thirtieth win of the season.
Above: Former Tigers' star McLain, at age 39, surrenders to Federal authorities to face rackateering and narcotics charges, in March of 1984.

2 OCTOBER 1968

Bob Gibson strikes out 17 men in the first game of the World Series

One of the greatest performances in that Year of the Pitcher, 1968, in which Denny McLain won 31 games and Don Drysdale pitched 58 and two-thirds consecutive scoreless innings, was turned in by Bob Gibson of the St Louis Cardinals, one of the hardest-throwing right-handers in National League history. Gibson spent all of his 17 major-league years with the Cards, winning more games for them than any other pitcher. He was five times a 20-game winner, fanned over 200 batters a record nine times and, nearly as overpowering as Sandy Koufax had been in his prime, set the league career strikeout record with a total of 3117. He took the MVP Award and one of two Cy Young Awards in 1968.

His ERA was 1.12 in 1968, the lowest for a pitcher with more than 300 innings in major-league history, breaking the National League record of 1.22 set by Grover Cleveland Alexander in 1915 and the American League record of 1.14 set by Walter Johnson in 1913. He completed 28 of the 34 games he started, winning 22, and was not once knocked out of the box. Gibson also led the league in strikeouts with 268 (allowing only 198 hits and 62 walks), won 15 games in a row, and threw an amazing 13 shutouts. Five of these shutouts were consecutive: over one 100-inning stretch, he allowed only three runs.

Despite his incredible performance during the 1968 regular season and his impressive career statistics, it is as a World Series performer that Gibson will always be remembered best, if only because it was in this venue that he received the greatest attention from the national media. Gibson set a Series record by winning seven consecutive games in 1964, 1967 and 1968, including three complete games against the Red Sox in 1967. But in 1968, to cap an astonishing regular season performance, he set a new Series record by striking out 17 men in one game.

Gibson faced the Tigers' 31-game winner Denny McLain in that well-publicized contest, but it was not one of McLain's better days. Gibson struck out two in the first inning, Dick McAuliffe and Al Kaline, and got Mickey Stanley out as well. In the second inning he struck out all three batters – Norm Cash, Jim Northrup and Willie Horton. By striking out Bill Freehan and Denny McLain in the third, he had fanned seven of the first nine batters to face him.

Gibson fanned Kaline again in the fourth and Don Wert in the fifth; he fanned two batters in the sixth, Stanley and Cash; and two batters in the seventh, Northrup and Freehan. Batting for Wert to open the eighth, Eddie Mathews became Gibson's fourteenth strikeout. By then the Cardinals were ahead 4-0, having reached McLain for three runs in the fourth and one more in the seventh. So far Gibson had given up only five hits and one walk.

Above: Bob Gibson hurling his magic from the mound.
Right: Strikeout victim number 16, Norm Cash stalks from the plate after being fanned by Gibson in the ninth inning of the first game of the '68 Series.

The partisan St Louis crowd was well aware at the top of the ninth that Gibson was within reach of the record of 15 strikeouts in one Series game set by Sandy Koufax in 1963. Mickey Stanley heightened the diamond drama by singling off Gibson to lead off the ninth, but moments later the crowd went wild when Gibson fanned Kaline for the third time and the scoreboard flashed the magic number 15. Cash next went down swinging and Horton went down looking, giving Gibson his 17 strikeouts and another shutout, 4-0. Gibson had fanned every man in the Tiger lineup at least once, giving up a total of only six hits and one walk. It was performances such as this that saw him elected to the Hall of Fame on the very first ballot in the first year of his eligibility, 1981.

15 SEPTEMBER 1969

Steve Carlton strikes out 19 players in one game – and loses

A pitcher whose record-breaking performances seemed only to improve with age, Stephen Norman Carlton, whose nickname 'Lefty' is a fitting reminder that he has struck out more batters than any other left-handed pitcher in major-league history, has often been called the finest National League left-hander since Sandy Koufax. A *New York Times* poll found him considered the best active major-league pitcher in 1983. By June of that year he had joined Nolan Ryan in passing Walter Johnson's magic mark of 3508 career strikeouts and by the end of the 1984 season Carlton – the only pitcher even to win four Cy Young Awards – had become the sixteenth member of that elite club of pitchers who have won over 300 games.

But his greatest single game, in which he achieved a feat that had eluded such greats as Rube Waddell, Lefty Grove, Christy Mathewson and Walter Johnson, was also a losing effort. On 15 September 1969 Steve Carlton struck out 19 players in one game. Out of 152 pitches he threw that day, he threw only two bad ones, but each one was hit by Mets outfielder Ron Swoboda for a two-run homer.

Carlton arrived at the ballpark for that game feverish and out of sorts. He required a rubdown and a painkiller for a sore back. But he struck out the first three batters he faced, and by the end of the seventh inning he had fanned the opposing side three times, logging at least one strikeout per inning, for a total of

14 strikeouts. The Mets had taken the lead in the fourth when Ron Swoboda homered with one man on, but the Cards had added two runs in the fifth to their one in the first, giving them a 3-2 lead at the top of the eighth.

Carlton added two more strikeouts to his tally in the eighth inning, but also threw his second bad pitch of the night, enabling Swoboda to hit another home run with one man on. By then Carlton was aware that he needed two more strikeouts to break the Cardinal team record of 17 in a game set by Dizzy Dean, and three more to break the major-league record of 18 shared by Bob Feller, Sandy Koufax and Don Wilson. To set a new all-time record he would have to fan three batters in the ninth inning.

Carlton started the ninth by slipping a fastball by relief pitcher Tug McGraw on a one-and-two count for strikeout number 17. The next batter up, Bud Harrelson, also fell to a fastball on the same count. He was strikeout number 18. Up next was Amos Otis, whom Carlton had already struck out three times. The count went to two-and-two. On the next pitch, a low slider, Otis swung and missed. Catcher Tim McCarver had to throw him out, but it was a strikeout, and Carlton had become the first to strike out 19 men in one game.

In the process he had struck out each man in the Mets' all right-handed starting lineup at least once; he had even struck out Ron Swoboda twice. But there was no arguing with the score. Carlton had lost the game, 4-3.

Sequence photos depict Cardinal left-handed ace, Steve Carlton's pitching style.

THE SEVENTIES

Brooks Robinson steals a hit from Johnny Bench in the World Series

In a career that spanned 23 years, Brooks Calbert Robinson set the modern standard for how third base should be played. His .971 lifetime fielding average is the best of any third baseman who ever played major-league ball; for 16 consecutive years he was voted the Golden Glove Award for best defensive third baseman. He also ranks first among third basemen in lifetime putouts, games played, lifetime chances and lifetime double plays. A dependable hitter, he six times hit more than 20 home runs.

But even such spectacular statistics pale beside his incredible five-game performance in October of 1970. Robinson hit .429 for the Series, tying a record with nine hits in five games (and four hits in one), and breaking a record with 17 total bases. But it is for his fielding, particularly the amazing diving catches that stopped Johnny Bench and others, that the Human Vacuum Cleaner will always be remembered. Robinson himself later remarked, '. . . I've never had five games like that in the 20 years I've been in baseball. During the Series I thought to myself, "I hope this gets over. It's unreal."' After the Series, the Hall of Fame acquired his glove for permanent enshrinement.

In game one at Cincinnati, Robinson's great plays at third included a backhand stab which robbed the Reds' Bernie Carbo of a solid hit down the third base line and an 'impossible' play off Lee May in the sixth inning that squelched a Reds rally. May shot a hard smash between Robinson and third base; after a few quick steps Robinson backhanded the ball when it was already past him and moving toward foul territory, then turned and fired the ball in one motion in time to get May out at first. Having stopped the Reds defensively, he then won the game with a home run in the seventh inning.

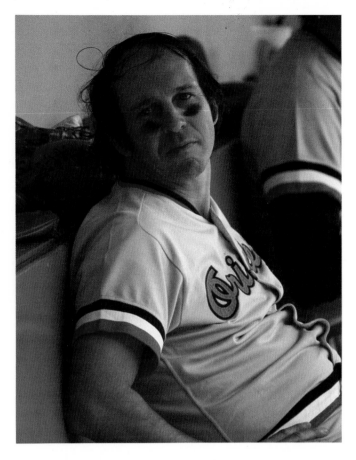

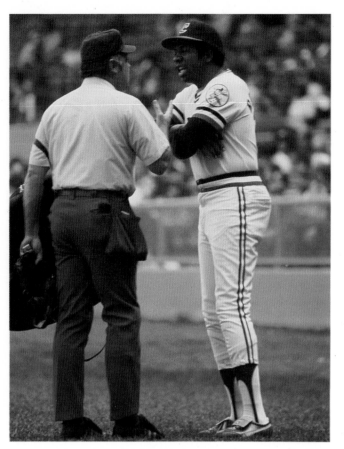

In game two Robinson made a diving stop of a Bobby Tolan smash, turning it into a force play, and in the third inning again stopped Lee May with a diving backhand grab that he turned into a double play. His bat drove in the tying run in the fifth.

Game three saw him make a leaping grab of a Tony Perez hopper that he turned into a double play, and he also beat out a Tommy Helms bunt for the out. It was in this game that he made his celebrated sixth-inning full-length diving stab of Bench's liner to save yet another hit. His bases-loaded double had driven in the Orioles' first two runs in the first inning, and he doubled again in the sixth.

In the fourth game Robinson tied a Series record with four hits, including a homer. The Reds won the game, 6-5, for their only victory of the Series, but Robinson helped his Orioles sew up the Classic in the fifth game with a final backhand catch of another Bench smash. It was Robinson's Series. Remarked opponent Johnny Bench, 'I never saw Pie Traynor play, but if he was better at playing third than Brooks, he had to be inhuman.'

Left: Brooks Robinson, stellar third baseman for the Orioles, in action on the field.
Far left: Johnny Bench, who led the league in homers and RBI's in 1970, cranks out a hit.
Above: Brooks Robinson rests in the dugout. Robinson was elected to the Hall of Fame in 1983.
Above right: At the end of his playing career, Frank Robinson became the first black major-league manager.

---

26 JUNE 1971

Frank Robinson's back-to-back grand slams

A hitter of tremendous power and a forceful, smoldering personality, in 1953 Frank Robinson announced his arrival in the major leagues with 38 home runs, tying the rookie home run record set by Wally Berger 31 years before. Chosen Rookie of the Year, he also led the league in runs scored, and wasted no time in establishing himself as a hitter in the same class with contemporaries Mays and Aaron, and perhaps the greatest hitter in Cincinnati history.

In 1961, with a slugging average of .611, the second of three consecutive slugging titles, Robinson was named the National League's Most Valuable Player. In 1962 he averaged .342 with 39 homers, 51 doubles and 136 RBI's; his fury on the basepaths earned him 18 stolen bases. But in 1965, when he was 30 years old, Robinson was traded to the Baltimore Orioles by a Cincinnati Reds team which labeled him 'an old 30.' Robinson promptly went to work for his new club, and in 1966 became the only player ever to be named MVP in both leagues, capturing the Triple Crown with 49 home runs, 122 RBI's and a .316 batting average.

Robinson also became the only player ever to have led both leagues in slugging percentage, and one of a handful to play on the All-Star squads of both leagues. He homered in more major-league parks (26) than any other player, his lifetime total of 586 homers places him fourth after Aaron, Ruth and Mays. To a career studded with firsts he added one more when he took over the reins of the Cleveland Indians in 1975, becoming the first black man ever to manage a major-league club.

Robinson had hit more than one home run in a game several times before 1971, but on 26 June at Robert F Kennedy Stadium in Washington he could not have expected very much of himself. The previous afternoon he had sprained his back making a spectacular game-saving catch against the Red Sox in Boston, and his usually powerful swing was greatly hampered by pain. To make matters worse, he had sat up until 4:00 AM the night before with his feverish seven-year-old son Kevin, and had had less than five hours sleep.

But in the fifth inning of the match with Washington his professionalism must have won out over his troubles. The bases were loaded – Dave McNally had walked, Don Buford had singled and Paul Blair had walked – when Robinson again came to bat against Joe Coleman, who had already stopped him twice. With two strikes, he went for a pitch that was a little outside ('I was afraid it might nick the corner . . .') and put it over the right-field wall.

In the sixth inning bases were again loaded when Robinson came to bat: McNally had again walked, Buford had singled and Blair had walked. With no apologies, Robinson launched a fastball thrown by Joe Grzenda into the upper left center stands for one of the longest homers of his career, adding a total of eight runs to the Orioles' 12-2 win. Six other players had hit two grand slams in one game and two had hit them in successive times at bat, but only Robinson had done it in successive innings. Questioned about his aching back after the game, he remarked, 'It hurts, but it didn't hurt enough for me to stay out.'

Roberto Clemente spirits the Pirates to World Series victory

In 1971 the Pittsburgh Pirates were the overwhelming choice to lose the World Series to a Baltimore Orioles club that was looking for its second consecutive world championship in its third straight Series appearance. The Pittsburgh team had terrorized the National League with an avalanche of home runs and a .274 team batting average, but the Orioles, fresh from winning their last 11 games in the regular season and three straight victories in the playoffs, were an experienced, well-balanced team with four 20-game winning pitchers.

No one was surprised when the Orioles took the first game, 5-3. Baltimore hurler Dave McNally held the Pirates to only three hits and set down 21 of the last 22 batters he faced. But two of those hits, including the only double of the game, came off the bat of Roberto Walker Clemente, one of the most abundantly gifted players ever to appear on a baseball diamond. In 18 years and 3000 hits with the Pirates he hit above .300 13 times and led the National League in batting four times; his powerful arm earned him five assist titles and the respect of baserunners. Of his performance in the 1971 Series Roger Angell wrote that Clemente displayed '. . . throwing and running and hitting at something close to the level of absolute perfection . . . playing the game almost as if it were a form of punishment for everyone else on the field.' By

Below: Frank Robinson at bat during the sixth game of the '71 Baltimore-Pittsburgh Series, 16 October 1971.
Right: Roberto Clemente at bat. Clemente's 12 hits in the '71 Series included two doubles, a triple and two home runs, with three runs scored and four RBI's.

the time the Series was over – the fourth game was the first Series night game, witnessed by 61 million television viewers – America had learned two things: the Pirates could win the Series, and Roberto Clemente, whose sustained seven-game performance has few parallels in Series history, was one of the finest players ever to grace a photon tube.

Game two went to the Orioles, 11-3. One columnist wrote of the Series, 'It's an atrocity; it's the Germans marching through Belgium.' But Clemente hit a single and a hard double against the right-field wall, and made a classic throw which, while it didn't win the game, let the Orioles know he was still there. Despite his performance, the Pirates were now two games down.

In game three in the sixth inning a Clemente grounder scored a runner from third and helped Pittsburgh to a 2-0 lead. The Orioles' Frank Robinson made it 2-1 with a homer in the seventh, but in the bottom of the inning Clemente broke the game open when he hit an easy grounder to pitcher Mike Cuellar, who was so astonished to see Clemente running at top speed into an easy out that he threw wide and Clemente was safe. Unnerved, Cuellar walked Willie Stargell, whereupon Bob Robertson missed a signal to bunt and hit a three-run homer. The Pirates won, 5-1, breaking the Orioles 16-game winning streak.

Game four saw another Pirate win in a close contest with Clemente getting two more hits, bringing his total for the Series to seven. The Pirates took their third straight victory in the fifth game, 4-0, Clemente driving in one of the Pirate runs with a clean single for a total of nine Series hits. He had now logged at least one hit in each of his previous 12 Series games.

Baltimore evened the score by winning the sixth game, 3-2, but not before Clemente knocked out a triple and his first Series home run, keeping the game as close as it was with a brilliant throw from the right-field corner.

In the seventh and deciding game Clemente stopped an Oriole rally with a running catch of a Frank Robinson fly ball, then sent a Cuellar pitch over the left-center fence to make the score 1-0. No more runs were scored in this tense pitchers' battle until the eighth inning, when Pittsburgh's Jose Antonio Pagan drove in Willie Stargell. The run was needed, because the Orioles, playing for a frenzied Baltimore audience, also squeezed out a run in the eighth. But Pirate ace Steve Blass retired three batters with eight pitches in the ninth, and that was all she wrote.

Acknowledged the Series MVP by the *Daily News* after the third game – and later officially – Clemente had totalled 12 hits, hitting safely in every game (as he had in the 1960 Series). His Series .414 batting average included two doubles, two home runs and a triple. Pittsburgh had their championship, and Roberto Clemente, to that date not as well-known as he would have been had he played on a team more frequently in the limelight, was at last recognized as a superstar by fans everywehere.

15 OCTOBER 1972

Joe Rudi saves one for the moustache gang

Under owner Charles O Finley, the 1972 Athletics were a hard team to take seriously. They wore gaudy green and gold uniforms, and many still sported moustaches and sideburns left over from one of Finley's great 1971 promotion ideas – players who grew moustaches received a bonus. True, the A's boasted such formidable players as Reggie Jackson, Bert Campaneris, Joe Rudi, Sal Bando and Gene Tenace, and pitchers Vida Blue, Catfish Hunter and Rollie Fingers. But only Rudi, at .305, had hit above .300 in 1972, and owner Finley – when he wasn't busy promoting orange baseballs and three-ball walks or two-strike strikeouts – quarreled with manager Dick Williams, played favorites and interfered with team play in perhaps more ways than any previous owner had ever found possible. Despite all this, Rudi, whom the A's had obtained from Kansas City in 1968, led the league in hits in 1972, with 181.

In 1972 the Athletics, in Oakland since 1967, won the first American League pennant the once mighty franchise had taken in 41 years. They were universally considered easy meat for the National League champions, the Cincinnati Reds. One of the fastest National League teams in decades, the Reds featured such future Hall of Famers as Johnny Bench, second baseman Joe Morgan, and the versatile Pete Rose. To make matters worse for the A's, Reggie Jackson had broken a leg sliding in the playoffs against the Tigers, and would be out for the Series; and Vida Blue, who had pitched a superb MVP-Cy Young year in 1971, had been virtually neutralized by the

Above: The Pirates' Roberto Clemente at bat during the fifth game of the 1971 World Series.
Below: Oriole pitcher Mike Cuellar lost the two Series games he pitched in the '71 Series.
Right: Dick Green tries unsuccessfully for the double play as Bench scores from third in the 1972 Reds-A's World Series.
Far right: Jim 'Catfish' Hunter pitched two wins in the '72 Series.

machinations of colorful owner Charles Finley. Blue had no qualms about saying that he felt Cincinnati and Pittsburgh, the 1972 National League playoff contenders, were both better teams than his; and the Reds were so confident of Series success that, according to writer Ron Bergman, 'they thought they'd win in three.'

But the A's did win, in one of the strangest and closest World Series contests ever, and went on to win three World Series in a row, a feat no other team except the Yankees has ever accomplished. Six of the seven 1972 World Series games were decided by only one run, and the A's team batting average was .207 to the Reds' .208. In a Series this lean – the spectacular performance of the A's catcher Gene Tenace excepted – shrewd management and consistent team play were

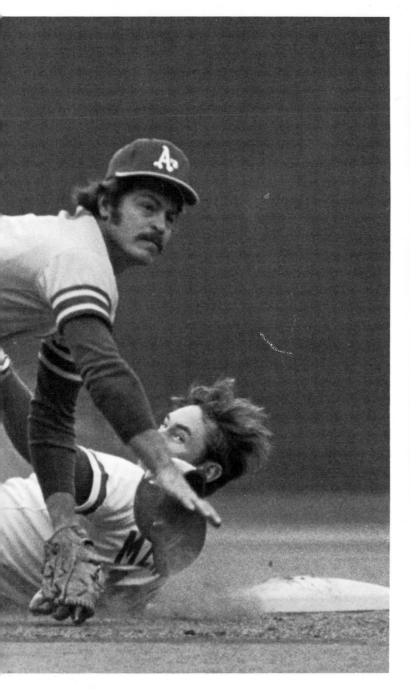

more important than individual performance. Every hit and every fielding play, every run and every game was important.

The A's took the first game, 3-2, in what the Reds considered a fluke. In the second game, which the A's won 2-1, Oakland showed what solid pitching and stout defense can do. In the second inning of that game, Oakland's Sal Bando, Dick Green and Catfish Hunter all singled to get one run across.

In the next inning Oakland's Joe Rudi hit a solo homer, bringing the score to 2-0, Athletics. Hunter had given up only four hits over the first eight innings, but Perez singled to lead off the Cincinnati ninth, and then Denis Menke hit Hunter's next pitch deep to left field for what looked like a home run that would tie the game. But Joe Rudi ran full tilt to the fence, looked

over his head, turned to the right and jumped at least four feet into the air, back-handing Menke's drive before crashing into the fence. He recovered, and kept Perez from getting further than second.

Manager Williams called it the greatest catch he had ever seen. Had Rudi failed to make the catch, the Reds definitely would have been back in the game, for Perez advanced to third on the next out, and finally did score off a single by pinch hitter Hal McRae. Hunter was then removed, and Rollie Fingers promptly retired pinch hitter Julian Javier for the final out. The Reds had now had a taste of the kind of persistent effort that would 'upset' the Series, but could not make the grade as they fell to the A's in seven games. It was to be the hallmark of Oakland play for the next two years as well.

BALL STRIKE OUT BATTER AVG
.15
1 2 3 4 5 6 7 8 9 0 R H E
TWINS 4 10 2
ANGELS 4 8 2

Nolan Ryan sets the all-time season strikeout record on his final pitch of the season

In 1974 Nolan Ryan, the fastest fastball pitcher ever clocked, became the first major-league pitcher to strike out 300 or more batters in each of three consecutive seasons. What makes him such a great strikeout pitcher is hard to pinpoint, but Sandy Koufax, to whom Ryan is most often compared, makes the point that 'Pitching is the art of instilling fear.' The more a batter is intimidated, the better; batters hate to face Ryan not just because of his fastball, but because his control is suspect. Reggie Jackson claims that Ryan is the only pitcher who puts fear in him, 'Not because he can get you out, but because he can kill you.'

In 1973, a year in which 12 American League pitchers won 20 or more games, Nolan Ryan won 21, threw two no-hitters and two one-hitters, and registered an ERA of 2.87. While the accomplishment of which he is proudest is his all-time record of five career no-hitters, it was in 1973 that he broke Sandy Koufax's record of 382 season strikeouts and set a new all-time record of 383.

Going into the Angels' last game of the 1973 season, against the Twins on 27 September, Ryan needed 15 strikeouts to tie Koufax's record. By the end of the eighth inning he had fanned his 15 players, but he was severely hampered in the ninth by a leg cramp. Between-inning massages from the trainer helped, but Ryan found himself unable to deliver his fastball with his best stuff. He was still looking for his record-breaking strikeout at the top of the eleventh, with the Twins and the Angels still tied at 4-4.

Two outs later, with Rod Carew on first base, he was still looking. Next up was Rich Reese. Ryan got two strikes on Reese, but after the second strike Carew took off for second base. Catcher Jeff Torberg made a good throw for the attempted putout, but Carew just managed to beat it out. Later Torberg confessed that although he had thrown instinctively and well, he had hoped Carew would be safe.

So it was that Ryan still had a chance at a new record. On his very next pitch he fanned Reese to end the inning. Reese was his sixteenth strikeout of the game but, more important, it was his three hundred and eighty-third strikeout of the season, and Ryan had set a new all-time record. As icing on the cake, Ryan's teammates pushed a run across the plate in the bottom of the eleventh, giving him his twenty-first and final win of the season.

Nolan Ryan walks from the mound as the scoreboard in the background tells the story of his record-setting strikeout number 383, 27 September 1973.

Hank Aaron's seven hundred fifteenth home run

It's only natural that the man who tied Babe Ruth's record lifetime total of 714 home runs and went on to set a new record of his own (755) should be compared to The Bambino, but no two men could ever have been more dissimilar. The quiet, methodical, efficient, consistent and self-effacing Hank Aaron once said of Ruth, the most dramatic of baseball players, 'Even if I am lucky enough to hit 715 home runs, Babe Ruth will still be regarded as the greatest home run hitter who ever lived.'

'Bad Hank's' assault on Ruth's record probably began five years before he was born, when his father, Herbert Aaron Sr, climbed a pine tree outside a ballpark in Mobile, Alabama, and saw Babe Ruth belt a legendary homer. The elder Aaron, who managed a baseball team called Aaron's Whippets, taught his son to hit bottle caps with a broomstick to develop his eye. By the time Hank was 14 years old, he was playing with grown men on the Whippets team. A pitcher who later faced him once remarked, 'Throwing a fastball by Henry Aaron is like trying to sneak the sun past a rooster.' 'I've never been a dumb hitter,' said Aaron, commenting on his approach to batting. 'It's confidence in what I'm doing. I'm either going to scare the pitcher to death by not hitting the ball, or hit it.'

Aaron slammed his first major-league homer for the Milwaukee Braves on 23 April 1954. Between 1955 and 1973, 'The Hammer' never hit fewer than 24 nor more than 47 home runs. His greatest single season was 1959, when he averaged .355 with 46 doubles and 39 homers, becoming the only National League player in the last 35 years to log 400 total bases. But he was a team player. The home run which gave him the biggest thrill of his career occurred in the eleventh inning of a game on 23 September 1957 – it gave Milwaukee the pennant.

On 10 June 1972 Aaron hit home run 649 and passed Willie Mays to become number two in lifetime homers behind Ruth. At this point he finally conceded that he might pass The Bambino if he stayed healthy. The next two and a half years 'should have been an enjoyable time, but everywhere I went people were talking about home runs. The lack of privacy was the main thing. . . . I couldn't go anyplace.' Aaron had to take all of his meals in his room; often the team rented two rooms for him – one under his name, and one unregistered, in which he stayed, protected by private guards. When hate mail piled up from racists who couldn't tolerate a black man breaking a white man's record, Aaron stopped reading his letters.

Aaron hit home run 713 in the second-to-last game of the 1973 season. In the last game of the season the 39-year-old got three clean hits and popped out, but no home runs, disappointing his fans. Still, it was

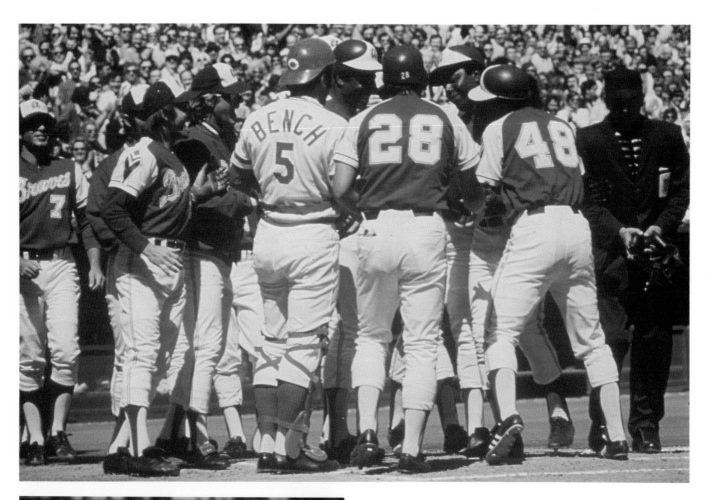

only a matter of time, and in 1974 the Braves' owners wanted him to sit out the first three games (scheduled for Cincinnati) to maximize his chances of tying Ruth's 714 homers in Atlanta. But Commissioner Bowie Kuhn overruled these machinations, and on Aaron's first swing of the 1974 season, on a pitch off Jack Billingham, he tied Ruth's 39-year-old record. It was his eleven thousand, two hundred eighty-ninth major-league at bat; Ruth had hit his 714 in 8399 at bats.

Four days later, on 8 April 1974, at Atlanta Stadium, before his mother and father, 53,000 fans, and an estimated 35 million television viewers, Henry Aaron hit his seven hundred fifteenth home run off a pitch from the Dodgers' Al Downing. Still deferring to Ruth, he said, 'It's the Cadillac of baseball records.' But it was his now, and Bad Hank went on to hit 755 home runs before he retired, establishing a record that will undoubtedly remain a challenge for some time to come.

Far left: Hank Aaron at bat prior to hitting home run number 714 to tie Babe Ruth's record on 4 April 1974.
Top: Hank Aaron receives some hearty congratulations after hitting home run number 715.
Left: Nolan Ryan, who led the league in strikeouts seven times, winds up for the pitch.

77

18 OCTOBER 1977

Mr October earns his name

When he came to the Yankees in 1977 at the age of 31 Reginald Jackson was already one of the most exciting and controversial figures in baseball. Like Babe Ruth, he was the highest-paid player of his day, and like Babe Ruth, he was a great slugger. To complete the picture, he was now a Yankee; but here the comparison ends. Jackson celebrated his first year as a Bomber with a Series performance that even Babe Ruth had never delivered. In the process, he set five new World Series records and created one of those moments that live forever in the minds of baseball fans.

Up to the 1977 Yankees-Dodgers Series Jackson's epic squabbles with Yankee manager Billy Martin and owner George Steinbrenner had made as much news as his play on the field, and his lackluster two hits in 15 times at bat during the playoffs with Kansas City held little promise of great things to come. After nine trips to the plate in the first three games of the Series Jackson had only two singles to show. But in the fourth game, with New York ahead in the Series two games to one, he got a double off Doug Rau and a home run off Rick Rhoden. The Yankees' Ron Guidry pitched a four-hitter for a 4-2 victory. In Jackson's final time at bat in the fifth game he clouted another home run as New York fell to the Dodgers 10-4. Reggie Jackson was beginning to wake up.

The Dodgers, trailing two games to three, got a 2-0 lead in the first inning of the sixth game. Los Angeles pitcher Burt Hooton, who had struck Jackson out twice and kept him hitless in the second game, walked Jackson his first time up (Reggie didn't swing once). But in his next at bat in the fourth inning, Jackson sent Hooton's first pitch into the stands with one man on, changing the score from 3-2, Dodgers, to 4-3, Yankees. The fans chanted 'Reg-gie! Reg-gie! Reg-gie!' until he came out of the dugout and tipped his hat.

In the fifth inning, on the first throw he received from relief pitcher Elias Sosa, Jackson hit one even harder into the right-field stands, driving Willie Randolph home and boosting the Yankees' lead to 7-3. Once again came the chants from the crowd and the traditional shower of rubbish with which New Yorkers honor their champions.

Yankee Stadium rose to its feet screaming when Jackson came to his fourth at bat in the eighth inning. At 10:51 PM, Jackson hit the first pitch from Dodger relief ace Charlie Hough 450 feet into the center-field bleachers. When he took the field for the Dodgers' ninth, so much rubbish was showered on him by adoring fans that he had to don a batting helmet for protection. The Yankees won the game, 8-4, and they won the Series.

Hitting .450 for the Classic, Reggie Jackson had set five new World Series records: most homers (5), most runs (10), most bases (25), most consecutive homers in one game (3) and, since he walked between his homer in the fifth game and his first homer in the sixth, most consecutive homers in official times at bat (4). Babe Ruth, the only other player to hit three homers in one World Series game, did it twice, in 1926 and 1928, but his shots were neither consecutive nor decisive. Reggie had also tied World Series records with three homers in a game, 12 total bases in a game, and four runs in a game. All his homers in the last game came on the first pitch – he took only three swings that day – and it is probable that no other player in major-league history has ever hit four home runs on four consecutive swings.

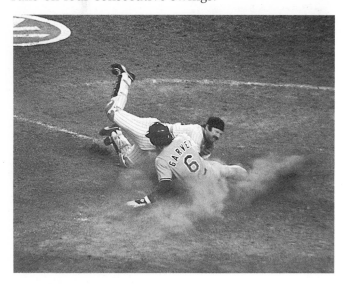

Left: Reggie Jackson belts a long ball.
Above: Steve Garvey is safe at home as Yankee catcher Thurmon Munson attempts the tag in the '77 Series.

2 OCTOBER 1978

The American League's most exciting playoff game

Never had there been such a pennant race. The Red Sox moved into first place in the third week of May 1978, and by 19 June they were eight games ahead of second-place Milwaukee. The Yankees, torn by epic squabbling among manager Billy Martin, slugger Reggie Jackson and owner George Steinbrenner, were 14 games out, in fourth place. But after Bob Lemon replaced Billy Martin on 24 July, the Yanks started to win.

In September, while the Yankees won 15 of 16 games, the Red Sox lost 14 of 17, including four in a row to New York at Fenway Park. By 16 September, the Sox were three and a half games out and sinking. But they came back to win 12 of their last 15 games, and tied the Yankees for first place in the Eastern Division on the last day of the season. The second one-game playoff in American League history was scheduled to break the tie.

Red Sox-Yankee rivalry had been a tradition for years. In 1904, 1938, 1939, 1941, 1942, 1949 and 1977 the two teams had finished in first and second place in the American League, the Yankees taking the pennant every year except 1904. The tradition continued in 1978. Pitcher Mike Torrez, sold by the Yankees the year before and opening for the Red Sox in the playoff, was looking to get even; the Yankees, starting Ron Guidry, accused Torrez of bad-mouthing them, and were also looking for revenge.

Boston's Carl Yastrzemski knocked a ball out of the park in the second inning for the first run of the game. Boston scored again in the sixth inning, bringing the score to 2-0 at the top of the seventh. Just as the Yankees had come back late in the season to become pennant contenders, they woke up late in this game. Chris Chambliss singled in the seventh inning, Roy White singled and Jim Spencer popped out, bringing shortstop Bucky Dent up to bat with two men on and one out.

Dent fouled the first pitch from Torrez smack into his ailing foot. While he shook off the pain, Dent was passed a new bat by next-up Micky Rivers, who sent word with the batboy that there was a home run in it. Against all odds – Dent had hit only four homers that year and was batting .140 in his last 20 games – Dent knocked one over the left-field fence to put the Yanks in front, 3-2. Then Mickey Rivers walked and Thurmon Munson drove him home, giving New York a 4-2 edge. The replacement of Guidry with 'Goose' Gossage in the bottom of the seventh ended a Red Sox rebound, and Boston did not score that inning.

Reggie Jackson added a home run to the Yankees' tally in the top of the eighth, but Boston fans went wild as the Sox added two runs of their own in the bottom, bringing the score to 5-4. With the Yankees retired quickly in the top of the ninth, excitement at Fenway Park rose in intensity. Three outs in the bottom of the ninth could decide the pennant – one run would tie the game.

Gossage walked Sox shortstop Rick Burleson, and with one out Jerry Remy lined to right. Thinking Lou Piniella would make the catch and unable to hear his third base coach waving him on, Burleson did not venture beond second. Piniella had in fact lost sight of the ball, but he was able to fake that he was about to catch it, then managed to stop it on the first hop, holding Burleson to second. Jim Rice then smashed a fastball to deep right. Piniella caught it and Burleson tagged up and moved to third. Had he been on third, he would have had plenty of time to reach home.

With one out to go and the tying and winning runs on base, Carl Yastrzemski, a great clutch hitter

Page 80: Chris Chambliss congratulates Reggie Jackson as he crosses the plate after hitting a home run on 18 October 1977.
Page 81: Red Sox catcher Carlton Fisk warms up in batting practice.
Below: Yankee fireman Rich 'Goose' Gossage held on to the Yankee lead in the exciting New York-Boston playoff game on 2 October 1978.
Right: Ron Guidry, the Yankee's starting pitcher in the playoff game, led the league in both wins and ERA in 1978.

who had hit the ball hard that afternoon, came to the plate. Gossage did not underestimate him: 'Yastrzemski's the greatest player I've ever played against.' The tension was unbearable. Gossage's first pitch was a ball. The second looked like the fastball Yaz was waiting for, and he swung hard. But the pitch rose slightly as it reached the plate, Yaz popped it high over third base, and Nettles caught it with no difficulty. The Yankees had won, 5-4, clinching the pennant to cap one of the great pennant drives in history, and contributing once more to the bitter tradition of Red Sox second-place what-if finishes.

Rickey Henderson steals his record-breaking one hundred nineteenth steal on a headfirst slide in Milwaukee on 27 August 1982.
Inset: Henderson holds aloft his stolen base number 118, with Lou Brock, in a mid-game ceremony.

27 AUGUST 1982

Rickey Henderson breaks Lou Brock's record on the way to a new all-time season record of 130 stolen bases

In 1915 Ty Cobb set a season record of 96 stolen bases, a record that lasted until 1962 when Maury Wills, then 29 years old, set a new major-league mark of 104. In 1974 Lou Brock, playing for the St Louis Cardinals, passed Wills and set a new season mark of 118. It took Brock, then 35 years old, 151 games to steal his 118 bases. In 1982 23-year-old Rickey Henderson, the third major-leaguer to pass Cobb's record, stole his one hundred nineteenth base in his one hundred twenty-ninth game of the season,

and before the season was over, set a new all-time season record of 130 stolen bases.

It takes a certain arrogance, as well as fearlessness, speed and knowledge of pitchers, to make a good base-stealer. Lou Brock, who saw some of Henderson's steals on replay in 1980, thought the kid had talent. According to Henderson, Brock, who still owns the career record for stolen bases with 938, '. . . came up and talked to me. He told me he thought I would be the one to break his [season] record. I was a rookie and it was a good feeling.'

In 1980 Henderson stole 100 bases, all from first to second, setting a new American League record. In the strike-shortened 1981 season he managed only 64, but in 1982, having made the discovery that he could also steal from second to third, he made it no secret

that he was going for Brock's record. On 2 August 1982 Henderson stole his one hundredth base and became the first player in history to compile two 100-steal seasons. On 4 August he got up to 104, and the media circus began.

On 26 August, in Milwaukee, Lou Brock and hundreds of media personnel were on hand as Henderson, the A's leadoff batter, opened with a single up the middle against pitcher Mike Caldwell. Knowing Henderson was hungry for his one hundred eighteenth steal, Caldwell attempted to hold him close to the bag with two soft throws to first. The count reached 1-2 on Dwayne Murphy, as Henderson extended his head and took off for second, making his famous headfirst slide. When second base umpire Durwood Merrill called him safe, Henderson leapt to his feet, raised his hands over his head, and tipped his hat to the 30,896 fans who were giving him a standing ovation.

Although he was disappointed that he had been unable to tie and break Brock's record in the same game, Henderson only had to live with the pressure of getting the record one more night. On 27 August, with two outs in the third inning, Milwaukee starter Doc Medich, whose slow, deliberate motion seemed made

for base-stealers, walked Henderson on four balls, then threw to first four times trying to pick him off.

Catcher Red Simmons called for a pitchout on the first pitch to Oakland third baseman Wayne Gross. Simmons rifled the ball to shortstop Robin Yount, but the throw was just a bit to the right of second base. Henderson, diving headfirst, was safe.

The ballgame stopped for about four minutes for a brief ceremony. Henderson, holding second base up for the crowd to see, invited teammate Dwayne Murphy, who usually batted behind him, to share in the celebration, claiming that he couldn't have broken the record without him. Manager Billy Martin passed out '119' T-shirts, Henderson shook hands all around, and made a brief speech with Brock and American League President Lee MacPhail at his side.

Then Henderson went out and stole three more bases for a game total of four and a season total of 122. Steal 119 had come on his one hundred fifty-eighth attempt; he had already been thrown out 39 times, breaking Ty Cobb's major-league record of 38 failed steals set in 1915. His teammates, allowing that he deserved a rest if he wanted one, praised Henderson's return to the game. According to Oakland pitcher Matt Keough, 'Nobody would have cared if he'd just walked off. Instead, he did some things that could have won the game for us. People should remember that.' Henderson went on that season to set the all-time season stolen base record of 130 in a display of cunning and speed never before, or after, equalled.

Left: Ty Cobb, the first great base-stealer of modern baseball, slides into base. Cobb's spikes were notoriously sharp.
Above: Rickey Henderson acknowledges the applause after his record-breaking steal.

Fireworks brighten the sky as teammates congratulate Pete Rose on first base after his record-breaking hit.
Inset: Pete Rose, attempting to break Cobb's record on 31 August 1985.

11 SEPTEMBER 1985

Pete Rose gets hit 4192 for a new all-time major-league record

Over two decades ago Whitey Ford derisively dubbed an over-achieving young ballplayer named Peter Edward Rose 'Charlie Hustle.' It was typical of the brash young rookie who ran to first base on walks and slid headfirst into bases, playing with an almost lustful joy, that his tenacity, resourcefulness and desire to 'play the game the way it's supposed to be played' turned the name into a badge of honor befitting an authentic baseball immortal.

Pete Rose, also known as the Record Man, played the game with all the fire and skill of Ty Cobb, but without his malice, thereby earning the love and appreciation of teammates and opponents alike. Along the way he became the personification of what athletes mean by 'desire.'

Rose began collecting honors and records in his very first season, when he was named 1963 Rookie of the Year. The all-time leader in major-league at bats, he has more seasons (10) with 200 hits than any other player. Beginning in 1965, he hit .300 or better for 14 of the next 15 seasons, taking league batting titles in 1968, 1969 and 1973. He also holds the major-league record for the highest lifetime fielding percentage by an outfielder (.992). The first singles hitter to earn $100,000, on 5 August 1979 he became the best singles hitter in National League history when he broke Honus Wagner's mark of 2426 singles. He was named MVP in 1973, Series MVP in 1975, and National League Player of the Decade and Athlete of the Decade for the 1970's. In 1981 he set another major-league record by starting at his fifth different position in the All-Star game.

Of all the records Pete Rose made or broke, his topping of Ty Cobb's 1928 mark of 4191 career hits most captured the public imagination. Rose got his first hit, a triple off Pittsburgh's Bob Friend, on 13 April 1963. In 1973, after he had already logged 1922 hits in his first decade of play, Rose allowed, 'I'm the only active guy with a legitimate chance to get 4000 hits.' No one disputed him.

He got his two thousandth hit, a single, off Ron Bryant of San Francisco on 19 June 1973. On 5 May 1978, at the age of 37, he became the thirteenth player in history to join the 3000-hit club when he got a single off Steve Rogers of Montreal. In the same year 'Pistol Pete,' hitting in 44 consecutive games to tie the National League record set by Wee Willie Keeler, came as close to Joe DiMaggio's immortal 56-game hitting streak as anyone has since the Clipper set it.

Hit number 3651, a single off Mark Littell of the Cardinals on 10 August 1981, broke the National League record for hits established by Stan Musial. On 22 June 1982, when he hit a double off John Stuper of St Louis for hit 3772, Rose moved into second place on the all-time hit list. In 1982, when he had completed his twentieth major-league season, Rose needed just 322 hits to tie Ty Cobb's all-time record of 4191 hits. At the end of 1983, he needed only 202 hits.

When Rose doubled off Philadelphia's Jerry Koosman on 13 April 1984, 21 years to the day from his first major-league hit, he became the second man in the history of organized baseball to compile 4000 hits. By the end of the 1984 season, he needed just 95 hits to break Cobb's record. Speaking as playing manager of Cincinnati, a club he had played on for 17 years, Rose said it was just a matter of time, and everyone knew it was.

Rose opened the 1985 season with two hits. From the beginning of the season a nation and a gradually swelling press corps began following Rose – at 44 the oldest regularly performing player aside from pitchers in the major leagues – as he closed in on the record. The 'Rose Watch,' as the press caravan came to be called, reported his progress to the nation the way it might follow a long countdown to a space mission. At least 225 journalists were on hand on 8 September 1985 when Rose logged hit 4190 and tying hit 4191, both singles, off Reggie Patterson of Chicago. His tying of Cobb's 57-year-old record made the front page of *The New York Times* and every major newspaper in the nation.

On 11 September 1985, in Cincinnati's Riverfront Stadium, 10 miles from where he began playing baseball as a boy, before a sold-out crowd and 300 journalists, Pete Rose broke Ty Cobb's mark in the first inning when he lined the fourth pitch from San Diego's Eric Show safely into center field. The stadium exploded, literally. Fireworks were set off and the ecstatic fans showered the field with streamers and confetti. Rose had gone to bat 2334 times more than Cobb to equal his record, but no one cared just then.

Teammates and well-wishers mobbed him at first base. Reds' owner Marge Schott kissed him and presented him a red Corvette. Rose removed his batting helmet and waved his gloves to the crowd, then threw his arms around old friend and batting coach Tommy Helms and cried. After the game President Reagan called to congratulate him. Banner headlines flew across the front page of every newspaper in America. Television appearances came later. The city of Cincinnati renamed the street that runs past Riverfront Stadium 'Pete Rose Way,' while in Washington, the Senate approved a resolution praising Rose for breaking Cobb's record.

Before the landmark game was over, Rose had gotten another hit, number 4193, a triple in the seventh inning. In typical fashion, he scored the only two runs of the game, leading his team to victory, 2-0.

Top right: Pete Rose takes a ball before making the landmark hit.
Right: Roger Clemens with his powerful release, pitching for a new record at Fenway Park.

29 APRIL 1986

Roger Clemens sets a new major-league record of 20 strikeouts in one game

In the 147,000 major-league games of professional baseball history no one had ever achieved the mark reached by Roger Clemens, a 23-year-old right-hander in his third season with the Red Sox, on 28 April 1986. On that fateful day Big Tex earned a place for himself in the record books as the first pitcher ever to'strike out 20 men in one nine-inning game. Bob Feller's modern record of 18 strikeouts in nine innings set in 1938 (a mark later equalled by Bill Gullickson, Ron Guidry, Don Wilson and Sandy Koufax) stood until 1969, when Steve Carlton bumped it to 19. Tom Seaver, facing no designated hitters, threw 19 strikeouts in 1970, followed by Nolan Ryan in 1974 (Charles Sweeny had thrown 19 strikeouts in nine innings in 1884). Ryan in fact threw four 19-strikeout games, but only one ended after nine innings; Louis Tiant struck out 19 in 1968, but in ten innings; and Tom Cheney, who holds the record for most strikeouts in one game with 21, did it in 16 innings, in 1962.

Clemens' career – and his record – almost didn't happen at all. In Clemens' first year with Boston, he got off to a brilliant start and was being compared with Dwight Gooden when he pulled a muscle in his right arm and was out for the season. Back again in 1985, he had a 4-2 record going in May when he began to experience weakness in his shoulder. Forced by pain to stop playing, in August of 1985 he underwent arthroscopic surgery for a slight cartilage tear in his right arm. A diligent worker, Clemens began doing weight exercises the day after the operation. Even so it was questionable whether he would ever pitch again.

Pitching coach Bill Fischer babied him through 1986 spring training, and Clemens himself didn't dare cut loose until his third game – and third consecutive win – of 1986. But when he did, he struck out 10 Detroit Tigers in six and two-thirds innings. 'I knew then that I was back where I thought I was headed two years ago,' Clemens remarked. 'I also think I'm throwing better now than I ever did.'

On the night of 29 April 1986 Clemens knew he was throwing a strong game against the Seattle Mariners, and he was aware that the crowd in Fenway Park was screaming every time he got two strikes on a batter with his 95-mile-an-hour fastball and cunning curves, but 'I wasn't sure what they were screaming about.' It was Sox pitcher Al Nipper who informed him at the bottom of the eighth inning, when 'Rocket' Clemens had fanned 18 Mariners, that he was only one strikeout away from tying the record.

The final score had been fixed in the seventh inning when Clemens gave up a homer to Gorman Thomas and Dwight Evans put the Red Sox ahead with a three-run homer. After the inning Sox manager

John McNamara asked Clemens how he was feeling. Clemens complained of leg cramps, then laughed to learn that McNamara was only interested in his arm. It was fine. Later McNamara commented, 'I watched perfect games by Catfish Hunter and Mike Witt, but this was the most awesome pitching performance I've ever seen.'

Clemens' legs still hurt when he came out for the ninth. 'I was pitching on all adrenaline at the time,' he said, 'and challenging them. I was throwing the ball right down the heart of the plate.' The fans, who rose to their feet for all of the ninth, watched him strike out Spike Owen, swinging, for number 19; and then Phil Bradley, looking, for record-breaking number 20. The third and last batter of the inning, Ken Phelps, hit a weak grounder to short for the final out, and the game was over.

It had been an awesome performance. Clemens gave up only three hits for his 3-1 victory and walked no one. Twelve of his strikeout victims went down swinging, eight called. He tied a record by fanning eight straight batters from the fourth to the sixth. He failed to get two strikes on only five batters, and only 29 of the 97 strikes (and 41 balls) he threw that day were even touched. Mariner manager Chuck Cottier said that the only other pitchers with his control were Bob Gibson and Sandy Koufax at his peak.

Above: Boston's 'Big Tex,' Roger Clemens, delivers to the plate during the first inning of the 1986 All-Star Game. Clemens' outstanding 1986 pitching performance helped his team to the Series, and won him both the Cy Young and MVP Awards.
Right: Boston's Rich Gedman blasts a home run at Anaheim early in game five of the playoffs.

Clemens had fanned Spike Owen, Phil Bradley and Ken Phelps in the first inning; Jim Pressley and Ivan Calderon in the second; Dave Henderson in the third; Bradley, Phelps and Gorman Thomas in the fourth; Pressley, Calderon and Danny Tartabull in the fifth; Henderson and Steve Yaeger in the sixth; Bradley and Phelps in the seventh; Calderon and Henderson in the eighth; and Owen and Bradley in the ninth, helping the Mariners to a new two-game major-league team strikeout record of 32.

No flash in the pan, the Rocket struck out 10 in eight innings in his next start, again giving up only three hits, and logged 14 consecutive wins before he was stopped. Clemens' 24 regular season wins propelled the Red Sox into the playoffs and helped galvanize public support behind a team that had had little to crow about during the last decade.

12 OCTOBER 1986

The fifth game of the AL playoffs

And just when it seems that there can be no more variations on the basic themes of baseball – no more surprises, no more great moments that haven't already been experienced – along came the 1986 playoffs and World Series. In the course of the 20 games that made up this post-season, there might be a number of candidates for the most crucial plays or hits, but most fans would agree that the fifth game of the American League playoffs, between the Boston Red Sox and the California Angels, was one of the most exciting games ever played.

To begin with, the Red Sox were not even supposed to be there – not if one listened to the sportswriters who had picked the Red Sox to end up in about fifth place in the Eastern Division. Instead, powered by the bats of Wade Boggs (who would take the league's batting championship with his .357), Jim Rice, Don Baylor, Dwight Evans and Rich Gedman, and inspired by the arms of Roger Clemens, Bruce Hurst and Oil Can Boyd, the Sox took over first place in mid-May and never yielded it. Meanwhile, the California Angels had moved ahead of the pre-season favorites, the Kansas City Royals, had held off a charge by the Texas Rangers, and had ended up taking the Western Division.

The first two games were played in Boston's Fenway Park, and the Angels took the first, 8-1, behind the superb pitching of Mike Witt. The Red Sox came right back in the second game with Bruce Hurst pitching, and routed the Angels, 9-2. The playoffs then moved west, where the Red Sox dropped the next two games. Now behind 3-1 in games, the Red Sox were everyone's favorite Eternal Losers.

When the Red Sox reported to Anaheim Stadium on Sunday, 15 October, even some of them might have wondered if they would not be better off in church. With the Angels' ace, Mike Witt, facing them on the mound, and being the visiting team, the odds were stacked against the New Englanders. But Boston was still in the game, with a 2-1 lead and with Bruce Hurst pitching, until the sixth inning. At that point the Angels' Bobby Grich hit a long ball. Center fielder Dave Henderson, who had joined the team in August (in a trade with the Seattle Mariners) ran to the fence, then leaped to make the catch. As Henderson smashed against the fence, the ball popped out of his glove and tipped over the wall for a two-run homer. Grich rounded the bases to the deafening applause of 64,223 fans, and the Red Sox dugout grew quiet.

In the next inning the Angels added two runs, and by the ninth inning the Sox were still trailing 5-2. In the Angels' clubhouse the champagne was moved out to be ready for the victors. Then Bill Buckner hit a single, and after Mike Witt got his first out, Don Baylor hit his curveball over the left-field fence. With the Sox trailing by one run, Witt got Dwight Evans out. As Boston's left-handed catcher came up to bat, the Angels' manager, Gene Mauch, had to make a crucial decision. Gedman had hit Witt effectively, so Mauch brought in the left-handed Gary Lucas, but the deci-

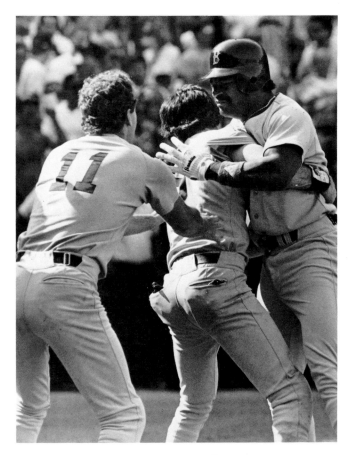

sion backfired when Lucas hit Gedman with his first pitch. Up came Dave Henderson, Mauch brought in Donnie Moore, and the Angels were soon one strike away from winning their first pennant ever. Moore tried the pitch that was foiling so many batters, the split-finger, but Henderson connected for a home run, giving the Sox a 6-5 lead. Red Sox fans across the country went wild.

In the bottom of the inning California tied up the game again when Rob Wilfong hit a ball to right, and Gary Pettis scored from second, sliding wide of Gedman's tag and touching a corner of the plate with his left hand. But the Red Sox reliever, Steve Crawford, pitched out of a bases-loaded, one-out jam to end the inning. Still tied in the eleventh, a hit batter and two singles loaded the bases with Red Sox, and Henderson hit a sacrifice fly that scored Baylor to put Boston ahead, 7-6. Calvin Shiraldi retired the Angels in order to end what Red Sox manager John McNamara called 'the best baseball game, the most exciting baseball game, the most competitive baseball game I've ever seen.' The Sox would go on to win the next two – and the pennant – at Fenway Park.

Left: Dave Henderson is greeted at home plate by teammates after belting his ninth inning home run.
Below: The ball pops out of Henderson's glove and over the fence in the sixth inning.

INDEX

Picture Credits

The Bettmann Archive: pages 9(bottom), 10(right), 11, 12, 15(bottom), 17(top), 18, 23(top), 32(top), 54, 55.
Chevrolet Motor Division: page 24.
Nancy Hogue: pages 68(left), 69(both), 78, 81, 83.
Ron Modra: pages 6(bottom left and right), 7(both), 82, 84(inset), 84-85, 87, 88-89, 91(bottom), 93.
National Baseball Hall of Fame, Cooperstown, NY: page 6(top).
National Baseball Library, Cooperstown, NY: pages 1, 8, 9(top), 10(left), 13, 14, 15(top), 16, 17(bottom), 19(top), 21(right and bottom), 29(top), 34(bottom), 39(right), 42, 45, 48(bottom), 52, 57(bottom), 58, 62(top), 64, 68(right), 73(right), 74, 86.
UPI/Bettmann Newsphotos: pages 2-3, 4-5, 19(bottom), 20-21, 22, 23(bottom), 25(all three), 26(both), 27, 29(bottom), 30, 31, 32(bottom), 33, 34-35, 36(both), 37(both), 38, 39(left), 40-41(all three), 43, 44(both), 46, 47(both), 48(top), 49(both), 50(both), 51(both), 53(both), 56(both), 57(top), 59(both), 60(both), 61, 62(bottom), 63(both), 65, 66-67(all three), 70, 71, 72(top and bottom left), 72-73, 76, 77(both), 79, 80, 88(inset), 91(top), 92, 94 (both).

Acknowledgements

The publisher would like to thank the following people who have helped in the preparation of this book: Adrian Hodgkins, who designed it; Barbara Paulding Thrasher, who edited it; Donna Cornell Muntz, who did the picture research; Cynthia Klein, who prepared the index. Special thanks go to Pat Kelly, Photo Collection Manager and staff at The National Baseball Hall of Fame and Museum, Inc; and to Katherine Graubard and staff at UPI/Bettmann.